your cat's just not that into you

# your cat's just not that into you

**richard smith**

author of *The Dieter's Guide to Weight Loss Before, During, and After Sex*

*illustrations by* david sipress

WORKMAN PUBLISHING · NEW YORK

Library of Congress Cataloging-in-Publication Data

Smith, Richard.
  Your cat's just not that into you / Richard Smith.
     p. cm.
ISBN-13: 978-0-7611-3947-8
ISBN-10: 0-7611-3947-8 (alk. paper)
1. Cats—Behavior—Miscellanea. 2. Human-animal relationships—
Miscellanea. I. Title.
SF446.5.S65 2005
636.8'0887—dc22
                                         2005048993

Interior Design by Patrick Borelli
Illustrations by David Sipress
Cover image by David Arky
Cat photo by Juliane Eirich

Workman Publishing Company, Inc.
708 Broadway
New York, NY 10003-9555
www.workman.com

Printed in the U.S.A.
First printing August 2005

10 9 8 7 6 5 4 3 2 1

# ACKNOWLEDGMENTS

For Paris, Nova, Sidney, and Hercules, as well as their owner-servants, Ken and Joanne. I also want to thank Ann and Matt, as well as my great editor, Richard Rosen, who constantly disabused me of the notion that cats think they're merely cats.

# CONTENTS

### 1. YOUR CAT'S JUST *NOT* THAT INTO YOU . . .
## IF SHE PRETENDS YOU DON'T EXIST

### 2. YOUR CAT'S JUST *NOT* THAT INTO YOU . . .
## IF SHE'S FAKING INTEREST IN YOU

### 3. YOUR CAT'S JUST *NOT* THAT INTO YOU . . .
# IF SHE PHYSICALLY ABUSES YOU

### 4. YOUR CAT'S JUST *NOT* THAT INTO YOU . . .
# IF NOTHING YOU DO PLEASES HER

## 5. YOUR CAT'S JUST *NOT* THAT INTO YOU . . .
# IF HE'S EMOTIONALLY UNAVAILABLE

## 6. YOUR CAT'S JUST *NOT* THAT INTO YOU . . .
# IF SHE TEASES YOU WITH OCCASIONAL MOMENTS OF PSEUDO-INTIMACY

## 7. Your Cat's Just *Not* That Into You . . .
# IF SHE TOYS WITH YOUR SELF-ESTEEM

## 8. Your Cat's Just *Not* That Into You . . .
# IF SHE FLAUNTS HER NEW LOVE INTEREST IN FRONT OF YOU

### 9. YOUR CAT'S JUST *NOT* THAT INTO YOU . . .
# IF SHE SHOWS NO RESPECT FOR YOU OR YOUR POSSESSIONS

### 10. YOUR CAT'S JUST *NOT* THAT INTO YOU . . .
# IF SHE GOES OUT OF HER WAY TO MAKE YOU FEEL OR LOOK BAD

# INTRODUCTION

My friend Rachel, cat lover and doting owner of two (a monster Maine Coon and a Persian), recently popped this question:

"Do you ever get the feeling that your cat is giving you mixed messages?"

"Like what?" I replied.

I knew where this was going, but why be cruel? As the "resident" cat expert among my friends, I've had a lot of experience with deluded cat owners. I listened to Rachel as I watched Dinah, my golden-haired tabby, ensconced on my desk, continue to pay no attention to me—her loving, adoring owner—preferring, instead, to nibble on a stack of unpaid parking tickets.

"Sometimes when Phoebe is rubbing against my leg," Rachel continued, "I can feel the love travel up my pantyhose. Then, suddenly, she walks away, as though our moment of intimacy meant nothing. Is she afraid to show her vulnerable side? Is she trying to tell me that—" Rachel began sobbing.

Is she the first owner to make excuses for her cat? Hardly. Believe me, I've heard them all: "Oh, she needs more time"; "He's withholding affection because of a difficult childhood"; or "She's still pining for the camaraderie of the animal shelter." And this, from one elderly gent who'd just made out his will: "I know that Emma, my Turkish Van, would love me unconditionally if she knew how much money I'm leaving her."

My own epiphany occurred years ago. Like most cat owners, I imagined I was the most fabulous owner on earth. What cat in her right mind wouldn't want to be owned by me? When Dinah and I walked down the street we made an amazing couple. I was happy to give Dinah unconditional love. "Is your dish the right color, darling?" "Do you need something to make you sleepy—some Johnny Mathis or a tureen of schnapps?" "Would you, my angel, prefer something softer to munch on, like my new running socks?" "Would you like me to join you in that tree?"

But there was a "love gap." When I got home, there was no Dinah waiting for me at the door, panting with delight, joyfully wagging her tail and meowing rapturously. Sometimes, she didn't even notice that I was there. When she saw me, I wondered, did she even know that I was me?

Was I making excuses for my cat? Of course she never came when I called her! I probably wasn't saying her name loudly enough. In the middle of her lap nap (my lap, her nap) when she suddenly leapt up and scampered away, she wasn't rejecting me! After all, she did have a right to visit her imaginary friend. Was she ungrateful? Never. She was just too shy to thank me for keeping her photo on my desk.

Oh sure, we'd play, we'd snuggle, she'd wake me in the morning with fish breath, but rarely did I get the feeling that any of this mattered to her. And so it dawned on me: When a cat is into you, she lets you know it. She wants to meet your friends, she can't keep her paws off of you, she's never too busy to sit next to you during the playoffs, she'll never yawn in your face, and when it's time for bed she doesn't care that you don't have designer sheets.

Did other cat owners want to hear this? Could they face the truth without drinking iodine? I started my website: *www.dateotherdeluded catowners.com* and soon the stories and complaints were pouring in:

> • "Even when she's on my lap, I get the feeling that Mambo, my Siamese, is wondering, *Is there a better lap out there?* Richard, is it my cellulite?"

> • "I think that Zeke, my long-haired Tuxedo, would 'open up' and love me more if he weren't traveling under an assumed name."

> • "Oslo, my Norwegian, knows I treasure my roses, but she eats the petals, anyway. And when I say, 'Bad Oslo,' she simply walks away. Why is she pretending she doesn't speak English?"

Okay, it's hard. We love our cats and we want them to love us back. Rejection can be painful. But accepting that your cat is just not that into you can be liberating. No more disappointment, no hoping you'll get what kitty can't give. You stop expecting things. Whatever she gives you—a mouse, a hair ball—you're thrilled she's at least showing some interest.

So are we all wasting time with the wrong cat? Should we cut our losses and move on to dogs? Or scrapbooking? Are there cats out there who would be that into us? Possibly. There was Pookie, the Grateful Cat of Athens, who dragged his owner by his toga out of a burning senate. There was Monet, who managed to tap out 911 with his paw when his owner started going bald. But these are exceptions.

What I can tell you is that it's a lot easier to think of yourself not as your cat's "owner," but rather, as the person your cat deigns to live with—her servant, if you will. Will that day come when your cat sees the light and is finally that into you? Perhaps.

Just kidding.

# Terms Used Throughout

- **CATTUS INTERRUPTUS:** That split second when, as you're cuddling with that warm, furry, purring creature called "your" cat and thinking, Ain't life grand?, she abruptly darts away to pounce on a passing dust bunny, thus ruining the mood and leaving you wondering, Will I ever learn my lesson?

- **KIT KAT?:** Any cat who comes in a kit. Imported from South Korea, easily assembled, and featuring nylon pile fur. Kit Kat is designed for owners who won't accept that their real cat is just not that into them.

- **FLEAS:** What some cats settle for if they can't make larger friends.

- **THE WINDMILL:** A frantic back and forth motion of kitty's head, generating up to 7,000 megahertz, indicating that she's not enthusiastic about swallowing the pill you're trying to give her. Telling her, "It's for your own good," or using a plunger, rarely works and shouldn't be attempted.

- **FINICKY:** A cat who finds the molecular structure of her Friskies substandard.

- **EVAPORATE:** What your cat's "mental image" of you does the moment you leave the room.

- **LOVE:** What your cat can't give you enough of. Frustrated owners often cut their losses by either publishing a personals ad or turning to golf.

- **"HERE KITTY KITTY":** The mating call of the deluded owner who thinks that his or her cat will appear promptly. One owner, after saying "Here kitty kitty" 22,000 times with no response, actually suffered a stroke, not realizing that his cat was away, visiting relatives in Ohio.

- **KIT LIT:** Any work of literature in which cats figure prominently. As of last count there were 76,499 books covering such topics as why cats paint, why they must pee so audibly, why there are no police cats, and the proper way to give a cat with digestive problems a Rolaids.

- **DOG:** Pet who is into you.

- **ARISTOCAT:** (often misspelled aristocrat). All cats are of noble birth, descending from the ancient Cat-Kings of Mesopotamia, beginning with Pharaoh Mittens, who ruled over the Upper Nile, the Lower Nile, and a small deli in Cairo.

# OWNER–CAT ETIQUETTE ALERT

For the purpose of this book, proper etiquette dictates that, when he's feeling affectionate, kitty kisses owner first and *then* goes and sniffs another cat's butt. Reversing the order and sniffing another cat's butt immediately before kissing you guarantees that your cat is just *not* that into you.

Chapter One

YOUR CAT'S JUST *NOT* THAT INTO YOU . . .

# If She Pretends You Don't Exist

*Actually, she knows you exist; it's just that
she has other things on her mind.*

Why is a cat so incapable of acknowledging, at least occasionally, her loving, doting owner? Hasn't she just a moment to walk over and lick your face, or to make the effort to turn her head and say "Hi?" Many owners make excuses for their cat by citing their insanely busy lives. *Of course she has no time for me, she's lying in the sun, or she's making the rounds of the house.* Other owners rationalize their behavior as a defensive reaction to a pre-ASPCA era when cats were used as everything from beasts of burden (pulling little milk carts in Germany) to the Fighting Cats of Rome who, in their wee gladiatorial outfits, were forced to amuse Caligula's in-laws. Who's correct? I hope reading the following pages will help you decide.

# THE "I GUESS HER MIND IS ON OTHER THINGS" EXCUSE

Dear Richard:

My Numkins is the best—the most beautiful, warmest, furriest, fuzziest, lovable cat in the whole wide world—and we often experience amazing chemistry. The only problem is that she's never completely "there" for me. A few examples: When I:

- Sought comfort after breaking up with my ex
- Was distraught and tried to "end it all" by jumping into the paper shredder
- Had the flu
- Needed consolation when I got the audit notice from that meanie IRS
- Asked her, after being abducted by aliens, to, "Hold me tight, I just need some closeness"
- Needed protection from a mime

She simply went about her business, walking over to me and rubbing against my leg only when she felt like it and making limited eye contact when I needed her most. I'm sure she's really into me, but I suspect that most of the time, her attention is focused on deep cat thoughts.[1] Am I deluding myself?

*Lois*

---

[1] *Why can't I sing like Pat Boone?*

Dear Starved for Support:

Don't be fooled. I say, trade in that self-centered cat and make space in your life for the glorious things you deserve, like cable TV, the Lord, a new car, a lover who is totally into you, or, if you discover you're feeling like crap without feline companionship, at least one of those new, sympathetic kitties who are also trained grief counselors.

Oh sure, your cat is busy. Not a moment in her insanely busy schedule to lick your face, rub your leg, or even cough up one measly tribute-to-my-owner hair ball. That's nonsense. No cat is that busy. If she can't take a break from her day—perhaps cutting her yoga lesson short—to sit before you and sing, "Achy Breaky Heart," consider finding a cat who will.

# THE "WHEN I'M CALLING YOOOOOOOOUUUUU" EXCUSE

Dear Richard:

I can't tell whether my cat is just not into me or playing hard to get. When she vanishes to some secret part of the house, I can spend hours calling, "Here kitty kitty, here kitty kitty"—but she only appears when she hears "Her" can being opened. I'm her owner! Tell me she's only playing hard to get. I'm insecure.

*Muriel*

Dear Muriel:

Kindly apply a cold compress to your forehead. Holding it there? Good. It'll help relieve the psychic pain experienced by so many owners when they're dissed by their cat. You see, honey, the right side of your cat's brain does hear you, but the left side of its brain is usually focused on a dozing termite or a piece of fallen chicken; during these moments, it couldn't care less whom it is owned by.

Note: In rare cases, an empathetic cat will spare its owner's feelings of rejection and abandonment by a) leaving a poop the size of a burrito on the couch or b) shedding all over the baby.

Love these wonderful creatures, dote on them, care for them, take them sailing, but remember: They are haughty, disdainful, arrogant, withholding, standoffish, moody, petulant . . . okay, enough adjectives. Cats are their own person and not into you. Even when the great Renaissance artist Raphael painted *Mittens Adoring a Flounder*, he couldn't get the cat to gaze with proper adoration upon the fish. Raphael had to *fake* Mittens' expression. Are you more talented than Raphael?

## STRAIGHT FROM THE KITTY LITTER

You deserve an affectionate, demonstrative cat. One who showers you with unconditional love. A cat who is always happy to see you. A cat with a heart of gold who'll comfort you when you're ailing and who, when you come home, joyfully wags her tail instead of angrily flicking it over some perceived slight—you yawned in her face or you failed to use the good china when presenting her saucer of milk. If you find a cat exactly like this, let me know.

# THE "MAYBE SHE HAS ATTENTION DEFICIT DISORDER" EXCUSE

Dear Richard:

Okay, okay, let me lay it out for you. I get home, go into the kitchen, and as I start to put away the groceries, I realize I'd like some company. Fine. The parakeet's asleep and the hamster has a fever, but I know my faithful cat, Gilgamesh, is somewhere in the house. Our conversation goes something like this:

"Gilgamesh, where are you?"

Silence.

"Gilgamesh, sweetie, don't you hear me?"

Silence.

"Gilgamesh, I have a surprise for you." (I bought her this stupid little bear at Wal-Mart; the clerk swore it made her cat her slave.)

"Okay, Gilly, where are you hiding?"

She finally makes her grand entrance, strolling in as though she has all the time in the world. And then what does she do? She simply looks around, makes a pass at the leg of the dining table with her vibrissa, then saunters over to the exact spot on the floor where the sun is streaming through the window and collapses in a heap of drowsy fur. I think she has Attention Deficit/Hyperactivity Disorder. I've a good mind to spike her food with Ritalin.

*Edna*

Dear In Dire Need of a Plan B:

I want you to kneel and clasp your hands. Now say Kattish, the prayer for all the poor cat owners who cling to the pathetic hope that their cat is even remotely into them. It goes something like this:

O *Great Kitty Father in the Sky, grant me the power to accept that, of all the things that are really important to my cat, my cat is most important to my cat. Furthermore, grant me the power to believe that I'm a catch and deserve to be with a creature who cares, who can't wait to see me and be with me, a significant other such as a devoted and loving boyfriend or, if he's also one of those withholding, emotionally stingy jerks, a big Saint Bernard who slobbers all over me and joyfully barks the moment I walk in the door.*

Finished? Good, you may get up now. It's time to feed the cat.

# Advisory to Wilma

I share your frustration, but it's really so simple. Your dog is obedient and does pretty much what you tell him because dogs are, essentially, a body affixed to a tail. Doggy exists to a) please his master, b) sniff other doggies, and c) scare off strangers selling aluminum siding. Cats, on the other hand, are unpredictable because they have so many moving parts, permitting them a full range of independence—from warm, loving fur ball, to tail-flicking curmudgeon, to psychotic drama queen in a matter of moments. Now take a sheet of paper and write the following:

1. Obedient dog.
2. Obedient cat.

Guess which is the oxymoron.

## Cat Personal

### ISN'T LIFE MORE FULFILLING WHEN YOU'RE HUMILIATED?

Let this hidden gem take advantage of you. Exploitive but lovable Scottish Fold, on the lam and traveling under an assumed name (Trigger). Had to run away from owner too insecure to be dominated, now seeks weak, docile mistress who likes to beg, bow, and do my bidding. Reply in confidence to Starfire,

**Box 444.**

# TEN WAYS TO SUCK UP TO YOUR CAT

**1.** Her birthday? Surprise her with a bouquet of flowers and a certificate to a cat spa.

**2.** Leave affectionate Post-its by her kitty litter. Three suggestions:

    a. "Guess who loves you the most."

    b. "Who's the best kitty in the whole wide world?"

    c. "Shall I compare thee to a summer's day?"

**3.** In the morning, get out of bed extra gently so you don't wake Miss Sleepyhead.

**4.** Give her a back tickle even if she didn't ask for one.

**5.** Play "I'm in the Mood for Love" the moment she enters the room.

**6.** Praise her in front of her friends.

**7.** Appearance counts. She's always grinning? Apply whitening strips to her teeth.

**8.** Let her sit in your lap when you do the stationary bike.

**9.** Pet her while you make sultry tiger noises. Hope she gets it.

**10.** Name your truck after her.

How effective are these measures? What part of "meow" don't you understand?

# THE "MAYBE SHE DOESN'T KNOW HOW TO SHOW HER GRATITUDE?" EXCUSE

Dear Richard:

Does a stray cat know that it's a stray, and if I take her in and give her a good home, with lots of love and plenty of food and caring, shouldn't she be extra grateful and show constant appreciation? She went from roaming the streets and eating out of yucky dumpsters to living in the lap (mine) of luxury. I mean, when I brought her home, I even carried her over the threshold, but so far, after three months, she disdains me and acts like she owns the place—she sleeps, she jumps, she stares out the window, there've been one or two tantrums, and a couple of times she disappeared overnight without leaving a note. Where's the adoration? The thank-you-for-rescuing-me-from-starvation? Don't I deserve more than one begrudging nuzzle and the occasional gust of bad breath? Is this her way of telling me that she prefers the wide open spaces?

*Glen*

Wait a Minute, Mr. Lonely Hearts:

Your cat is supposed to be aware of the fact that she was a stray? Yep. I'll bet she was wandering the streets, thinking, *Gosh, I'm a stray, life is tough, wish some kind stranger would find me and take me home.* Bulletin for Glen: Cats don't even know that they're cats, let alone are fussy about where they come from. Internal monologues are simply not their forte. True, after an especially juicy and satisfying field rodent, certain cats may labor under the delusion that they're either a jaguar or a sophomore at Yale, but generally speaking, cats are pretty much content to be cats and that's why your new cat is not—yes, I'll say it again—that into you. Consider trying to get her to feel closer to you by lighting a few bath candles and inviting her into the hot tub.

# THE "MAYBE OUR TAN IS THROWING HER OFF" EXCUSE

Dear Richard:

Here's what happened: We boarded our cat while we went on a round-the-world cruise on the QE2. During that time, we missed her and thought of her often. We even sent her postcards and once, from Cancún, we actually called the kennel to say hello. When we finally got back after six months, she not only didn't acknowledge us, she didn't seem that eager to reconnect and come home. She finally did leave with us, but only after we let her say goodbye to the many new friends she made. When we got home, there was no *so glad to be back* look on her face, even though we brought her a fish from Madagascar and made her favorite dish (Fix-in-a-Flash Kasha Popovers). We feel rejected and bereft. What did we do wrong?

*Dan and Vivian*

Dear Perhaps to a Cat You All Look Alike:
What you did wrong was to be born a human being. Your second mistake was not to have a dog. Hate to tell you this, but dogs bark, drool, and lose sanity points if you leash them for five minutes while you go inside a store. For cats, it's pretty much, "out of sight out of mind." They don't wonder, *Where, oh where is my owner? Will he or she ever return?* All is not lost, however. Cat psychiatrist Amadeus Reich suggests you show how much you love her by making sure her serving dish is warm at feeding time. If that doesn't work, buy a backup cat, one who was voted Most Likely to Succeed at the animal shelter.

News flash! To a cat, all owners look alike. Whether you're gone three hours or three years, your cat's long-term memory is even shorter than her short-term memory. One cat owner, after doing a five-year stretch for embezzlement ("I did it for my cat"), came home expecting a warm greeting and a hearty handshake. Guess what: When you were arrested, by the time they slapped the cuffs on you, your cat no longer knew you. I say give those little tasseled loafers you made in the prison shop to a cat who cares.

Why do cats love to stare out the window? It's so simple: They're sadists. They like to watch people go to work, while thinking, "There but for my being a gorgeous, furry nonhuman with a doting owner, go I."

## THE "SHE'S JUST DAYDREAMING" EXCUSE

Dear Richard:

When she's not sleeping, my cat, Tut-Tut, can sit for hours, just staring out the window and looking at the sky. Sometimes she moves her head, but sometimes she's as still as the Sphinx, as though expecting something (she is, by the way, a sphynx). It is during these times that  she's even less that into me than usual. I have heard that cats can "sense" things that we humans can't, like earthquakes, hurricanes, and in-laws coming for dinner. Do you think she's awaiting the Messiah?

*Leslie*

Dear Leslie,

The Messiah? Perhaps. Either that or she's channeling J. Edgar Hoover. Of course cats can sense and hear things we humans can't. We often hear of super-clairvoyant cats sitting motionless, their ears cocked, listening to either radio waves from San Francisco or to a banana ripening. And there's Herb, the famous fire cat, who kept sensing smoke and dragged his sleeping owner from a burning building (alas, the owner eventually died of insomnia). It's certain that a cat sitting in front of a window has forgotten about you and being owned. (It is interesting to note that during one freezing winter, a cat scan of a sadistic cat revealed that he stared out the window only to enjoy the sight of pedestrians slipping on the ice.)

P.S. A sphynx? What does it feel like to cry on a bald shoulder?

# THE "MAYBE HE NEEDS TO TAKE IT SLOW" EXCUSE

Dear Richard:

A few weeks ago, after dumping my boyfriend, I decided to replace him with a loving, gentle, state-of-the-art, totally-into-me cat. At the animal shelter it was love at first sight: I picked up this golden, furry creature and he was all over me. He practically said, "Let's blow this firetrap," and when we left, didn't even wave goodbye to the other cats. But now that he's home, he's taken over the place and sometimes it's as though I don't exist. Salsa sleeps whenever and wherever he wants (trust me, this cat is not an insomniac), then suddenly flies around the place as though he's trying to rack up bonus miles. He often disappears and avoids eye contact when I ask where he's been (although he smiles and is suddenly extra-nice to my bird). His purrs shake the walls, and he practically ravishes me when I smear sardines all over my hands, yet he backs off or ignores me if I approach him empty-handed. Where's the love? Where's the romance? I'm thinking of cutting him out of my will.

*Donna*

Dear A Woman's Home is a Cat's Castle:

Have you tried mood music? Frank Sinatra? Hootie and the Blowfish? Look, dear, preowned cats, alas, often come with baggage, especially the cats sold on eBay. Perhaps Salsa was in a toxic and destructive relationship with a castrating Siamese or a selfish Persian. Perhaps he still has emotional scars from a futile love affair with an Afghan. You must therefore give him time and allow him to love and trust you at his own pace. Right now, he wants you for food, shelter, and a warm place to sleep. Be your cat's friend, by all means, but look for romance elsewhere. Like a boyfriend or a gnome who really knows what he wants.

Would your cat be more into you if you practiced "tough love"? If, say, you kept your mouth pressed tight when she kissed you, or showed her who's really boss by closing the hide-a-bed with her still in it? Probably not.

# THE "MAYBE SHE'S JUST NOT SUCH A GOOD LISTENER" EXCUSE

Dear Richard:

I've been with Elixir, my Norwegian mix, for three joyful years. We watch TV together, cuddle, and sometimes play with string. She loves to sit on my lap, and when we sleep, she's warmer than an electric blanket.

I feel so loved at these times. The problem is that, when I say, "Here kitty kitty, here kitty kitty," sometimes until I'm blue in the face, she never comes. Once, it turned out she was engrossed in the sports section or something. Why doesn't she report to me immediately?

*Renee*

Dear Sergeant Renee:

Please pay attention. If you want a pet who comes when called, get either a Labrador retriever or a needy lover. Does she hear you? Of course. But when she hears her name, the first thing kitty thinks is, How bad will it look if I scamper right over there? Will I appear subservient? Submissive? Meek? Docile? Worst of all, what will my peers think: Will I lose my standing as a cat?[1] Your cat, when called, may appear to be mutinous, but that's her nature. Ask yourself: Do you really want a cat who "yesses" you all the time?

[1] *We guarantee that your cat thinks of all these things.*

# Test Your Cat I.Q. (Basic)

1. Which of the following *does not* complete the sentence:
   Your cat never met _____ she didn't like.
   *a.* an anchovy
   *b.* a war veteran
   *c.* an accountant
   *d.* a nap
   *e.* a warm stoop
   *f.* Chinese takeout
   *g.* a tuna casserole
   *h.* a sunbeam
   *i.* a puddle of milk
   *j.* a tank top
   *k.* a disco fiend

2. Which one of the following sentences is false:
   *a.* When it hears its name called, a cat will always come at
      once.
   *b.* There is no such thing as an insubordinate cat.
   *c.* When on duty, a cat fends off sleepiness by slapping its
      face with an open paw.
   *d.* A cat pooping in front of a pit bull means five years of
      good luck (twenty years of excellent luck if the pit bull
      sniffs it).
   *e.* Cats prefer an owner who can make a perfect daiquiri
      from scratch.
   *f.* Outgoing cats hone their social skills by joining the Elks.
   *g.* If it has low self-esteem, a cat waiting to be adopted
      believes that all the good owners are already taken.

ANSWERS: 1. K 2. All the sentences are false except B, which is outrageously false.

## Chapter Two

YOUR CAT'S JUST *NOT* THAT INTO YOU . . .

# If She's Faking Interest In You

*Because if she's really interested in you, when you get home, she'll ask you about your day.*

Do her lips tell you *no no*, but there's *yes yes* in her eyes? You think that she's gazing at you with worship and adoration? Sorry, poor deluded owner. Cats are brilliant at getting what they want and do not consider it a violation of feline ethics—in fact, they think nothing of it—to fake a purr or pretend to be fascinated with your silly piece of lint, if it helps them get what they want. And, as the heartbreaking letters that follow illustrate, one of the primary things they want is to not be that into you.

# THE "BUT MY CAT THINKS I'M SUCH A GOOD CATCH(ER)" EXCUSE

Dear Richard:

Whenever I'm in the bedroom with Jed, my incredibly fun-loving Ragdoll, we play a game: I toss him in the air and he lands on the bed. Then, instead of running away or curling up on the pillow and dozing off, he leaps off the bed and into my arms as if to say, "That was fun, do it again." We have a great time together. So this time, Richard, I'm afraid you're wrong. It's obvious that Jed is into me; otherwise why would he keep coming back again and again until I have to lie down and fan myself?

*Max*

Dear You've Been Playing Hooky from Our Owner Obedience Seminars:

Yes, you're lucky to be with an exciting cat who makes you *feel* needed, but I hate to burst your bubble: Your game has activated the usually dormant reptile portion of your cat's brain, which, during the Jurassic period, enabled the cat to leap on passing dinosaurs and get a free ride to the nearest conifer. Your cat would be equally delighted if you placed him on a merry-go-round horse or luggage carousel and let him go around and around until the authorities hauled you away.

# Advisory to Mona in Dallas

Cats are vain, and it's natural, after your cat Phoebe discovered her first gray hair, to be upset, especially if she has liver spots on the backs of her paws. Explain to her that all of us, owners and their cats alike, must deal with life's misfortunes, like aging, grease fires, and using the lavatory of a Greyhound bus. My advice? Be sensitive to Phoebe, as she's kind of fragile right now. Stroke her with a basting brush and talk to her in a soothing voice but don't be too indulgent. How will she show her appreciation, you wonder? Is there still some part of "meow" that you don't understand?

# Red Flag Alert!

## WHAT CATS REALLY MEAN
## WHEN THEY SPEAK

| PHRASE | WHAT IT SHOULD MEAN | WHAT IT REALLY MEANS |
|---|---|---|
| *Meow* | Oh, my beloved owner, you mean more to me than anything else in the world. | **I'm just not that into you.** |
| *Mee-ow* | Dearest owner, feeling your closeness, your warmth, your adoration makes me feel like the luckiest cat in the world. | **I'm just not that into you.** |
| *Meow, meow, mee-ow* | I love our moments of intimacy, those times when it seems like the universe stops and it's just us, together, all cozy and fuzzy. | **I'm just not that into you.** |
| *Purr, meow* | Such a comfy lap does my owner have. Do you, precious owner, not see the bliss in my eyes? I could sit here forever. | **Nope, not that into you.** |
| *Purrrrr, meow* | Let me call you sweetheart, I'm in love with you. | **Not that into you.** |
| *Meow, purr, meow* | I would never do anything to make you feel bad, rejected or like one of those owners who exists only to feed their cat. | **Just not into you at all.** |
| *Meow, purr* | I spend my day counting the minutes until you get home, when my world lights up, and I am spiritually renewed. | **Couldn't be any less into you.** |
| *Meow, purr, purr* | Your fondles, your pets, the way you say, "Here, kitty," are nourishment to my soul. | **I'm just—how can I say it?— not that into you.** |

# Advisory to P.T. in Tulsa

Just because you are always there for your cat doesn't mean he'll always be there for you. It's not that he doesn't want to be. It's just that cats, being super-intelligent, have a lot on their minds, like "What am I going to do with my life?" or "Why is my dopey owner saying, 'Here, kitty,' when he knows perfectly well that my name is Nathan?"

Owners, please remember: When you love your cat, it's very tempting to think that it's "gifted," that it can do things no other cat can do, like waltz, or notice when you've had your teeth cleaned. ("Hello, Lucy? Can you believe it? Prism, our Bengal, is lip-reading *Silas Marner.*") The hard part is realizing and accepting that your cat's greatest gift is this: not being that into you.

A good rule of thumb: Just because your cat, or your blind date for that matter, exhibits human characteristics doesn't mean they are human.

## THE "BUT SHE REALLY IS TALENTED" EXCUSE

Dear Richard:

I'm a concert pianist. My friends think I'm crazy, but when Masha, my three-year-old Angora, "walks" across my piano keyboard, I swear she's picking out Bach's "The Well-Tempered Clavier, Book II, Prelude and Fugue No.3 in C-Sharp Major (BWV 872)." Not perfectly, of course (she's never had a lesson); she hits lots of wrong notes with her tail and sometimes her tempo sucks, but it's definitely Bach. Doesn't this prove that she's into me (and extremely gifted)?

*Wanda*

Tweet! Tweet! Ten Minutes in the Cat Co-Dependency Box for Wanda:

Is it possible you're hearing things? You may be gifted (or delusional), but not Masha. There have been just two truly musical cats: 1. Django, the Giggling Cat of Prague, who played Chopin on a Jew's harp and 2. Hermann, the minstrel of Brooklyn, who was lynched by the neighbors for playing reggae on the bagpipes at 3 A.M. As for Masha being into you through her "music," and thinking she's actually banging out Bach by walking on the keys, might I suggest you take a long vacation. Preferably someplace where it's quiet.

# Don't Despair

Time-tested secrets to make your cat a little less not that into you:

- Be there when she's having a bad day.
- Stop practicing karaoke in front of her. Cats find this annoying.
- Make her feel part of the family. At dinner parties, encourage your guests to feed her when she jumps up onto the table.
- Give your cat a real home instead of a small baby blanket in the toaster oven.
- Allergic to cat hair? Don't make it obvious by sneezing in front of her. She'll feel rejected.
- When exasperated at her, don't throw it in her face about how great your previous two cats were.
- Make her feel needed. If you're experiencing chest pains, allow her to fetch the defibrillator. Afterward, if you're not dead, pat her butt and say, "Good cat."
- If she plays hard to get, back off. This teaches her that you're no pushover.
- If she fails to rid your place completely of mice, don't accuse her of slacking. She may be honing her technique on roaches.
- Praise her when she does something wonderful. Did she intervene when you were cornered by a dentist at a singles bar? Hiss ferociously at an Amway rep? Be generous with her reward. (Extra catnip? New sunglasses?)

When they're in the mood, cats make wonderful playthings. They're light, easy to toss around, love to laugh, and, if you're extra-nice to them, many cats will, using their incredible powers of perception, alert you to underperforming stocks.

# THE "BUT SHE DOESN'T REALIZE I'M CONSTIPATED" EXCUSE

Dear Richard:

Talk about an insecure cat. I live in a small studio apartment and sometimes need my privacy. But whenever I go to the bathroom, my cat, Daisy, gets separation anxiety if I don't leave the door ajar. If I close it all the way, instead of wishing me good luck, she sits outside emitting meows, sometimes even scratching on the door (she gets frantic if she hears the lock snap). Once I emerge, however, instead of giving me a glad-to-see-you're-back, I-love-your-company expression, she just calmly walks away and returns to her search for wisdom by staring at the Glade PlugIns. Are her feelings hurt because I shut the door? Does she think I'm never coming out? I've never spent more than two hours in the bathroom so it couldn't be loneliness. I understand that many security firms have guard cats who are trained to sit outside corporate headquarters, inspect badges, and sound a meow alert if a nonemployee tries to enter. Could I have somehow gotten one of those?

*Edgar*

Right, Edgar:

And the Internal Revenue Service checks your return with error-sniffing cats. Daisy is manifesting that most confusing of all afflictions: Super Independent Cat Syndrome. A cat suffering SICS is definitely into you, but only when you're not there. She can express love only through a closed door. Do you deserve more? Yes, but good luck getting it. If you absolutely need privacy when you use the bathroom, but can't bear to hear your cat crying, you can either call her on your cell phone or simply slide your photo under the door while saying, "Hi, Daisy." She won't know the difference.

Kitty historians tell us that a cat's profound indifference to humans began in ancient times when, after conquering enemy territories, Hittite slave auctions featured not just humans. Slave cats in little shackles were sold to the highest bidder and used for everything from guarding harems and pulling chariots to wearing tiny wizard hats and predicting the future. Although these cats were treated well, they unionized and decided, "Why be into someone who makes us work so hard?" The rest is history.

# CAT ADOPTION CHECKLIST

Checklist for adopting kitty. Before giving a kitty a home, ask yourself:

✓ How many do I already have?

✓ How long will she last? Does she come with a warranty?

✓ Would I be just as happy borrowing my neighbor's cat when I'm lonely?

✓ Will I love being bossed around?

✓ Will I be able to swallow hard and say, "Good Kitty," when she destroys a 200-year-old heirloom?

✓ Am I ready to come home and find my cat having sex with a shoe brush?

✓ Will she "get it" when, for Halloween, I dress her up like a cat?

✓ Will she be appreciative when I stare at her little face and sing "You Are My Sunshine"?

✓ Am I comfortable with owning a creature whose primary source of fiber is socks?

✓ Am I ready to lavish attention, feed, care for, and support a creature who's a) not tax deductible and b) just not that into me?

# THE "UNABLE TO FACE REALITY" EXCUSE

Dear Richard:

You're not so smart. Other cats may jerk their owners around, but my cat is not only into me, she's *that* into me. Whenever I open a tin of cat food, she drops whatever she's busy doing, emits a loving meow, rushes over to the exact spot where I'm standing, and as I'm putting her bowl down, licks my fingers before chowing down. Doesn't that prove she's into me?

*Felicia*

Dear In Denial:

Yes, of course you're correct. Your cat breaks the sound barrier to get to her bowl because she finds you and your fingers irresistible. Her food?

A minor concern.

Three reality checks for Felicia:

· I will not assume that I am more important to my cat than her food.

· I will assume that my cat is licking my fingers because they smell of cat food, not because I just had my nails done.

· I will assume that I'm the apple of my cat's eye only if that apple smells like tuna.

# THE "IS IT IDENTITY THEFT?" EXCUSE

Dear Richard:

Is it possible to adopt a cat twice? About two years ago, I decided that Moona, my Burmese, was so just not into me (everything had to be on *her* terms; I don't even think she knew my last name) that I brought her to an animal shelter and kind of traded her in for a boyfriend. Then, last month, I decided I was just not that into my boyfriend, dumped him, and decided to adopt another cat. In the meantime, I had moved to another city, so I went to their local animal shelter and asked if they could show me something in a cat. Well, I fell in love with another Burmese, one who looked so much like Moona that I called her Moona-Two. To cover myself, I asked the people at the shelter if I could return her if she didn't love me, but they said, "Sorry, no trial offers. Cats leave here 'as is.'" Guess what? Moona-Two is also just not that into me. I want to be understanding, but after three weeks, she's just like my Moona One. When she licks me, I don't get that wet. She does pretty much whatever she wants, and when we go out, she walks several feet in front of me. Is it possible that I got the same cat again, and if I did, do you think she knows it's me?

*Walter*

Dear So Many Cats, So Little Time:

You've heard of the dog who traveled 7,000 miles from Tokyo to Dallas to find its owner? Here's what really happened: Moona was probably so just not that into you that, when you gave her away, she so missed being not that into you that she tracked you, much like a tiger stalking its prey. How did she know you moved? How did she know to be at the exact animal shelter that you were going to? The answer is simple: A cat has not just a sixth, but also a seventh, eighth, and ninth sense. Take the famous Catmandu Rescue Cats of Nepal, for example. Given EMT training and outfitted with a teeny barrel of brandy around their neck, they are taught to search the snow-covered mountains for lost climbers and, upon encountering a victim, emit vigorous meows until found by a search party. You're lucky. In her own way, Moona missed you and made a huge effort to be reunited with her beloved owner. Feel free to drop the "Two." (Caution, however; counterfeit Burmese from China abound.)

# THE "BUT MY PLANTS NEED WATERING" EXCUSE

Dear Richard:

Ethical dilemma time: About three weeks ago, my neighbor borrowed my garden hose, a Valentine's Day gift from my boyfriend. Is it wrong to hold his cat hostage until he returns it? I'm giving her a loving home and tie her up only at night. Please answer soon. I think we're falling in love.

*Amber*

Dear Amber:

There's nothing as wonderful as requited love. You're on cloud nine, you smile all the time, and there's a song on your lips. Unfortunately, this never happens with a cat. A cat does not care who "owns" it so long as it's fed, watered, and permitted to thrive. You're the one in danger of getting your heart broken if your neighbor returns your hose.

Do cats take their owners for granted? The real question: Do cats know they have owners?

## Chapter Three

Your Cat's Just *Not* That Into You . . .

# If She Physically Abuses You

*Unless she atones for your wounds
by fetching your slippers.*

Oh, you'll make excuses. You'll think, "He didn't realize his claws were extended," or as you gaze at the welt on your arm, "She didn't know the strength of her own tail." Or you'll excuse the bite that actually made an exit wound by rationalizing that kitty loves you so much he tried to "bite you to pieces." I know this is only Chapter 3, but, dear owner, it's never too early to start to face reality.

# Quiz: Know Thy Kitty

**1. Circle the answer or answers that apply. The classic symptoms of cat depression are:**

*a.* Sadness

*b.* Inability to sleep without a night light

*c.* Constipation

*d.* Low libido

*e.* Loss of appetite

*f.* Passivity

*g.* Wearing a shower cap

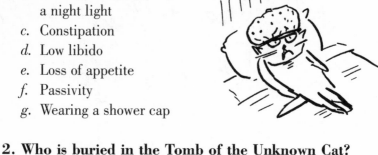

**2. Who is buried in the Tomb of the Unknown Cat?**

*a.* Freckles the Fierce

*b.* Abigail the Haughty

*c.* Cynthia the Great

*d.* Henry the Arrogant

*e.* Cuddles the Gladiator

*f.* Richard the Cat-Hearted

*g.* Lawrence the Lordly

*h.* Mittens the Fearless

*i.* Vincent the Salamander

ANSWERS: 1. Okay, class, raise your hands. How many answered E? I see four hands. Okay, how many answered A? Seven hands. Anyone circle C? Sorry, the answer is none of the above. Cats never get depressed unless: A. Their owner is sitting in their favorite spot on the sofa. B. They are forced at gunpoint to listen to Yanni. 2. The answer is i) Vincent the Salamander. They couldn't bear to inter a cat.

# THE "MAYBE SHE'S JUST TRYING TO GET UNDER MY SKIN" EXCUSE

Dear Richard:

Why is it that sometimes when I'm fooling around with Cindy, my Burmese mix, she scratches me? At first I thought she was being playful, but one especially deep, two-inch scratch left me thinking that she either a) doesn't love me anymore or b) for some strange reason wants a DNA sample. And when I hold up my arm and say, "Look what naughty Cindy did," she acts as though she hasn't the slightest idea who Cindy is or what I'm talking about. I heard that cats, being fussy, don't dig their claws into just anybody. Is there hope for me? Is she just acting out some queen of the jungle love fantasy?

*Paula*

Well, Boo Hoo Miss Sensitive:

A little scratch and you're all upset. You never heard the song, "You Always Hurt The One You Love"? Throw on a tourniquet, Paula, pour yourself two fingers of iodine, and listen up. Do you really think Cindy would go through the trouble of extending her claws and expending the physical energy needed to break your skin if there wasn't an ulterior motive? Cats are possessive. She's marking you as "Hers," much like a man giving a woman a hickey, except in your case you don't have to wear a scarf to the office the next day.

# Official Not-That-Into-You Word Jumble

### TIME LIMIT: 8 MINUTES

*1. Teriveces* _____

*2. Egila* _____

*3. Dudlyc* _____

*4. Gusm* _____

*5. Blimen* _____

*6. Giniddife* _____

*7. Volabel* _____

*8. Rudop* _____

*9. Strempset* _____

*10. Elfs-dretcene* _____

*11. Grotarna* _____

*12. Pendedentin* _____

*13. Techeadd* _____

*14. Sybso* _____

*15. Pluflay* _____

## HOW YOU RATE

0–5 correct answers: You get a cardboard star.

6–10: You get a hamster wearing a sheriff's badge.

11: Go ahead and get a cat, if you must.

12–15: You no doubt already have several.

ANSWERS TO WORD JUMBLE: 1. Secretive 2. Agile 3. Cuddly 4. Smug 5. Nimble 6. Dignified 7. Lovable 8. Proud 9. Tempetess 10. Self-centered 11. Arrogant 12. Independent 13. Detached 14. Bossy 15. Playful

## For Cats Only: What Owners Want in a Cat

1. *Owners want a natural cat.* They're turned off by the cat who dyes her fur and shaves her legs, unless she's wearing fishnet stockings.

2. *Owners don't like finicky eaters.* A cat who turns up his nose because the moth isn't precisely room temperature may find himself in reform school.

3. *Owners want a talented cat.* A gifted painter, for example, or one who sings tenor in a glee club. And the cat who can wrestle an enormous rat to the ground and make him cry uncle can name his price.

4. *Owners don't like the conceited cat who sells fur balls on eBay.*

5. *Owners don't like the cat who rolls her eyes when told about the high cost of gourmet cat food.*

6. *Cats love to laugh and owners prefer the cat who can take a joke.* Does dozing kitty laugh when owner sneaks up on her with the vacuum cleaner?

7. *Owners want a loyal cat, one who, for example, makes a show of being insulted if the mailman hits on her.*

8. *An owner prefers the cat who's flexible.* The cat who rejoices when her owner takes her front paws and does the samba is ideal.

9. *Being a thoughtful cat goes a long way.* Good kitty should keep a lid on the meows if owner has a hangover.

10. *Owners want the cat who respects private property.* The bulimic cat who projectile vomits should do so in a potted plant. (Disclaimer: Such nourishment may or may not enable plant to grow to full maturity.)

## What Do Owners Get in a Cat?

1. *None of the above.*

# THE "SHE DOESN'T REALIZE IT'S FOR HER OWN GOOD" EXCUSE

Dear Richard:

Talk about noncompliance. When I try to give my cat a pill, instead of obediently sitting there and, like a good patient, opening wide and swallowing, she turns her head, snarls, struggles, tries to pull away, and gashes my cheek. The pill is for her own good, right? So I think she's expressing that wish to remain ill, which Freud discusses in *Feline Invalidism in Frankfurt-am-Main* (University of Tony Press, 1922). Agree?

*Sam*

HERE
KITTY
KITTY!

Dear Sam:

Get a bible. Got it? Good. Now hold up your right hand and swear you'll never become an animal psychiatrist, especially the kind who actually has the animal lie on a couch and free associate. You see, my friend, what your cat is expressing is simply this: "My Dear, Darling Owner: Having my jaws pried apart by hands, no matter how loving, is not the way to get on my good side. I'm a CAT! I do not like doing what I'm told, and I hate being manhandled. Plus how the hell am I supposed to know that a pill the size of your prostate is for my own good? Next time, what do you say I pry *your* jaws apart and make you swallow a ping-pong ball? Let's see how you like it.

P.S. And don't ever try to give me an enema."

## CAT PERSONAL

### YOU ORDER THE PIZZA, I'LL ORDER YOU.

If you're submissive, read on. Upbeat, Rubenesque Maine Coon seeks good home with endlessly giving, insecure owner who'll try to please me even when I'm having a hissy fit. The right owner will never assume he's doing too much for his pet, or experience moral outrage if I "get lucky" with a gopher. Let's have lunch and talk.

**Contact Beowulf, Box 455.**

# YOUR FIRST CAT

A few Do's and Don'ts when you bring home your new kitty:

| DO . . . | DON'T . . . |
|---|---|
| . . . make her feel extra-welcome by wearing a nightgown with a cat motif. The sight of familiar faces will assure her that she's among friends. (Does she know they're actually cats? The debate goes on.) | . . . assign her sleeping quarters. Instead, let her roam and discover where she'll be most comfortable. It enhances her innate sense of independence and starts her on the road to being just not that into you. |
| . . . immediately begin calling her by her name. The cat with a past will feel like she finally has someone in her life who cares. Later, if she doesn't like it, she can always change it. | . . . spoil her too soon by constantly telling her how cute she is. Cats live for this and realize, after several mushy encounters, that you're completely besotted and will do anything for them. Telling her how cute and sweet she is once an hour is plenty. |
| . . . use trial and error to determine her favorite foods. Cats are finicky eaters, especially those prone to acid reflux; they'll turn up their nose and walk away rather than eat something subpar or "repulsive." Russian Blues, for instance, should never be offered pre-tasted caviar. | . . . make her feel too welcome too soon. She'll take advantage, and go from lowly cat to Serene Highness in two days. If you must, give her a little kitty greeting card that, when opened, plays "Memories" from *Cats*. |
| . . . make your cat pull her own weight. This helps her to "grow" and be the responsible cat she was meant to be. You need a second opinion on those earrings? Ask Fluffy. Need cheap prescription drugs? Buy a teeny backpack and a bus ticket, and send Fluffy to Canada. | . . . insist on teaching her tricks. This is not the way to a cat's heart. Cats are curious and intelligent beasts, preferring to experiment with life and learn things on their own. Have patience. I chuckled when one owner told me about coming home and discovering Percy, her Siamese, standing on her hind legs on the kitchen counter juggling dinner rolls. |

# THE "SHE MUST PREFER THE REAL ME" EXCUSE

Dear Richard:

My cat, Sadie, usually cuddly and affectionate, always loved to lie on my chest: I mean it was like her second home. But since I got home last week from the hospital, she'll lie on my stomach or my legs. Whenever I try to get her on my chest, she gives me a funny look, goes *tsk-tsk*, and scampers away. Do you think she knows I had implants?

(I went from a 32AA to a 38DD.)

*Hillary*

Dear Surgically, But Not Mentally, Enhanced:

Cats are adaptable, but not that adaptable— even the dumbest cat knows the difference between a mountain and a molehill. You're going to have to give Sadie time to get used to the new you, especially if, when she approaches your "new" chest, she hears sloshing. Will she ever be as that into you as she was before your "enhancement"? Guess what: Sadie never was that into you in the first place.

# THE "MY CAT'S JUST NOT THAT INTO ME" EXCUSE

Dear Richard:

    I hardly take care of my cat. Yes, I occasionally feed her, provide a ratty old bathrobe (chenille) for her naps, watch her sleep if I'm bored out of my skull, and last Halloween I dressed up in the Catwoman's leather body suit (she didn't get it). But the truth is, we lead very separate lives. I'm constantly busy with friends, two children, a high-energy career, and a Swedish chat room. My cat, Titto, on the other hand, totally ignores me. She dozes for what seems like months at a time, eats, hangs out in the laundry hamper or on the patio, and on occasion, hooks up with the cat next door. Does she miss me when I'm gone? Does she even know I'm alive? Not with her social life. So why should I make an effort to meet her even half way? Richard, guess what: I think she's just not that into me.

*Ivana*

Wow! Move over Diogenes:
 At last an honest cat owner. I'm shocked. You, Ivana, are a rare breed—you don't buy into the I'm-the-center-of-my-cat's-universe fantasy so prevalent among certain owners who cross that fine line between love and subservience, and actually check with their cat before redoing the kitchen or cutting their bangs.

## Advisory to Glenda in Little Rock

Any cat who insists that you play "Hail to the Chief" after he uses the kitty litter sounds like a petty tyrant. This is normal for a cat who, as a child, you say was bullied mercilessly by wild geese. You can try to modify your cat's behavior by:

1. Forbidding him to lie in the sun
2. Removing him as beneficiary of your SEP-IRA
3. Popping bubble wrap by his ear

# Red Flag Alert!

## THE OFFICIAL EARLY WARNING WRONG CAT DETECTION CHECKLIST

Cat expert Graham Pimlim, author of *Your Cheatin' Teeth*, lists the signs:

☐ *Does she use you as a doormat?*

☐ *Is she moody?*

☐ *While you gently blow in her little ear, does she flick it in annoyance instead of reciprocating?*

☐ *Does she get all sulky if she's having a bad hair day?*

☐ *Is she never "there for you" when*

   *a) The love of your life dumps you?*

   *b) Your computer crashes?*

☐ *Does she turn into a drama queen if you have less time for her because you met a new love?*

☐ *Does she have any idea where her grandparents are buried?*

☐ *Will she even notice if you're abducted by aliens?*

☐ *When you start to give her a back rub does she suggest you take a cold shower, instead?*

☐ *Does she get all pouty when you make her fly coach?*

**HOW YOU RATE**
If you answered all of the questions "yes," you're with the wrong cat. If you answered all of the questions "no," you're still with the wrong cat.

## Chapter Four

YOUR CAT'S JUST *NOT* THAT INTO YOU . . .

# If Nothing You Do Pleases Her

*Yes, cats are hard to please. I've yet to meet
the cat who is thrilled with her passport photo.*

So you assume that she won't wear the darling little Victoria's Secret nightie because it itches her skin. At her fourth birthday party, she ignored you totally and played with her friends. You truly believe that she'll stop sleeping in the guest room and sleep with you once you get over the measles. Well, dear owner, keep at it—we're sure your HMO covers cat owners who go crazy trying to please their cat.

# HOW PREDICTABLE IS KITTY?
## The Five Great
## Behavioral Equations

### 1. BOLTZMAN'S PRINCIPLE OF LEAST ACTION:

$$SoC \ x \ WoSB + HM = FRM$$

**APPLICATION:** Determining Kitty's resistance to being moved

**TRANSLATION:** SoC (sleepiness of cat) multiplied by WoSB (warmth of sunbeam cat is basking in) plus HM (how much cat has had to eat) equals FRM (force required to move cat)

### 2. MANNHEIM'S SPECIFIC THEORY OF MAGNITUDE:

$$C = 2\pi r$$

**APPLICATION:** Ascertaining your cat's true size.

**TRANSLATION:** C (circumference of cat) equals two times Pi multiplied by r (radius of the cat)

### 3. PLANCK'S OTHER EQUATION:

$$D = W \pm SoH \ x \ LoH$$

**APPLICATION:** Measuring how far a cat at rest can suddenly jump

**TRANSLATION:** D (distance) equals W (weight of cat) plus/minus (take your pick) SoH (size of automobile hood that cat is dozing on) multiplied by LoH (loudness of horn)

# 4. BLITZBERG'S SECOND LAW OF FELINE GRAVITY:

$$V = HoK \; x \; SoM \div VoS$$

**APPLICATION:** Calculating the speed of a falling cat

**TRANSLATION:** V (velocity) equals HoK (height of kitchen counter) multiplied by SoM (size of morsel cat was nibbling on without your permission) divided by VoS (volume of voice when you say, "Scat!") (Note: Add + 5 if cat has a guilty look.)

# 5. NEWTON'S FIFTH LAW OF DEVOTION:

**APPLICATION:** Determining how much your cat really loves you

a) Owner places dish of sardines in one corner of room

b) Owner places cat in middle of room

c) Owner goes to corner of room opposite sardines

d) If cat goes to owner, cat loves owner this much: 4974.28

e) If cat goes to sardines, cat loves owner this much: .0000000000002

## THE "WHY CAN'T WE ALL JUST GET ALONG" EXCUSE

Dear Richard:

I have a boyfriend who insists that kitty litter smells. The minute he comes over he starts sniffing the air and making yecch-type noises. He says he loves me, wants to marry me, and would move in with me in a minute (he's currently living in his car) if I did something about this "problem." My five cats think it's all in his head. What should I do?

*Daniela*

Dear In Need of a Breath of Fresh Air:

Get a new boyfriend. This one's jealous of your cats. As any cat will tell you, there's no such thing as smelly kitty litter. Ask yourself what you value more: Five fascinating, furry, occasionally loving, little companions or one tedious, finicky boyfriend who will not let you bring the cats on your honeymoon.

# Advisory to Eleanor

Does your cat care that you make a lovely couple? Does he love to stand beside you in front of a full-length mirror and admire how wonderfully the two of you complement each other? Sorry, Ellie, but cats don't need a human to tell them how gorgeous they are. Rare is the male cat who does not consider himself a hunk, even if he doesn't work out that often and has a beer gut. However, your plan to establish a learning center to make cats more aware of what their owners do for them is admirable. Calling it "Meow Helper" is a stroke of genius.

# THE "MAYBE THE ATMOSPHERE WASN'T RIGHT" EXCUSE

Dear Richard:

Is it possible that my cat, Lancelot, loves sushi more than he does me? The other night, to celebrate his fifth birthday, I went to a Japanese restaurant and brought home a very expensive assortment of fish. I assumed, before he began to eat, that he'd at least acknowledge the trouble I went to—a kiss, an intimate rub, jubilant drooling. Imagine  my surprise when he chose to show his appreciation by tearing into that sushi like Henry VIII inhaling a deer haunch. I didn't know his little teeth could move that fast. Don't try to tell me this wasn't a sign of deep gratitude.

*Joan*

Dear Put On Your Obi and Listen:

Unbelievable. A cat who'd rather gorge himself on tuna, yellowtail, and shrimp than take the time to make nice to his owner? I'm thunderstruck. But don't despair. I assure you that, as kitty stuffed himself, he was thinking nothing but nice and appreciative thoughts about how his giving, wonderful owner had schlepped home an entire sushi boat just for him. I also suspect that after he finished stuffing himself, he looked up at you with those beautiful cat eyes and asked, "What! No green tea ice cream?"

It is interesting to note that before castles had central heating, cats were prized for their warmth. Rare was the bed that didn't contain—in addition to a lord, several vassals, a serf, a goat—five or six cats, all chosen for their luxurious fur and solemn promise not to toss and turn during the night.

# THE "DO YOU THINK BEING A PARENT CHANGED HER?" EXCUSE

Dear Richard:

    Do cats really appreciate what you do for them? This year, when Matrix, our three-year-old Persian, gave birth to a litter of kittens, we made a really big deal over it. We gave her a cozy place to nurse them, we made a fuss about how cute and healthy they looked, and we took a photo and made it the screen saver for our main computer. Here's the heart-  wrenching part—on Mother's Day, for our little first-time mother, we baked a small cake and made her a special card in Photoshop. Instead of eating the cake, she took a teeny sniff and walked away. Our card? She never even acknowledged it. I know cats are not supposed to be *that* into us, but some gratitude, a "Hey, thanks for the cake and card," would have been nice. Do you think she's deliberately impolite or just wasn't raised properly?

*Tammy and Mandy*

Dear Daydream On, Girls:

Being a new parent changes people, not cats. They may be that into their offspring, but still not that into you. It sounds like you may be just a little jealous because Matrix is lavishing attention on her offspring rather than you. But remember, she's under a lot of pressure: getting her kittens weaned and walking, providing for their education, braces for their teeth, etc. Matrix won't be that into you for a long, long time . . . until, perhaps, she experiences empty-nest syndrome.

## CAT PERSONAL

### CAN YOU DEAL WITH A CAT WHO THINKS?

Vivacious kitty (former star of the Ice Catpades, currently a Baroque cellist) wishes to connect with deferential and obedient owner who will wake up each morning thinking, How can I make my cat's life better and happier?

**Call 1-900-Tuff Cat; hang up if a man answers.**

# ARE YOU YOUR CAT'S PUNK?

## TAKE THIS LITTLE TEST TO SEE HOW INTO YOUR CAT YOU ARE:

**You think about your cat 26 or more times daily.**

☐ *Yes*
☐ *No*

**While shopping, you pass a pet boutique and think how amazing those little cat moccasins would look on Esmeralda.**

☐ *Yes*
☐ *No*

**Do you write little poems to your cat on 3x5 cards and leave them where she can see them?**

☐ *Yes*
☐ *No*

**Do you generally spend more on gourmet cat food than the GNP of Togo?**

☐ *Yes*
☐ *No*

**To maximize kitty's comfort and give her more room, you bought a king-size bed.**

☐ *Yes*
☐ *No*

**Do you sleep more soundly and experience higher quality dreams when kitty is sleeping next to you?**

☐ *Yes*
☐ *No*

**Besides her real name, you have a secret pet name for her.**

☐ *Yes*
☐ *No*

**When at work you call your answering machine so she can hear your voice.**

☐ *Yes*
☐ *No*
☐ *Don't have to, I bring her to work in a picnic basket.*

**You pass on a night out with friends if you suspect your cat's feeling blue.**

☐ *Yes*
☐ *No*

**You cut up her salmon into tiny pieces just the way she likes it.**

☐ *Yes*
☐ *No*

**You've dumped a lover because he or she wasn't a cat person.**

☐ *Yes*
☐ *No*

**The essential phrase, "Cat Lover Preferred," is part of your on-line profile.**

☐ *Yes*
☐ *No*

**In your wallet you have 50 or more photos of your cat.**

☐ *Yes*
☐ *No*

**HOW YOU RATE**
Even one yes indicates you may be a slave to your cat.
Which is exactly the way she wants it.

# THE "BUT MAYBE SHE NEEDS MORE TIME" EXCUSE

Dear Richard:

If, at bedtime, my cat is already under the covers, must I ask permission to join her? She never actually invites me, and she doesn't really perk up or seem that thrilled when I slip in beside her. I know you're not supposed to sleep with a cat who breaks your heart, but I love her. I'm sure she'll come around and welcome me with open paws when she realizes what a neat and loving owner I am. Right?

*Carol*

Dear Sleeping Beauty:

The worst thing an owner can do is take her cat for granted. Not only may she not care whether or not you get into bed, she may not even know that warm, flannel-clad body is you. I say, ask her permission. It's a nice courtesy, and shows that you consider her your boss.

# THE "SHOULD I BE UNSELFISH AND CHANGE MY LIFE FOR HER?" EXCUSE

Dear Richard:

I lead an incredible life. My wealthy boyfriend showers me with expensive gifts; I have a marvelous job that takes me to Paris, London, and Rome; I earn enough to buy great clothes and live in a terrific apartment; and I have wonderful friends. The only problem is Sir Cat, my cat. I love him, even though an Egyptian Mau is not the most fashionable cat, but all he does is eat, sleep, leap, and doze. Do you think that my fabulously upscale lifestyle makes him feel depressed about his own drab life? Should I tone down my life a bit? I recently felt so guilty that I took him along and let him sit on my lap during *Rigoletto* at La Scala.

*Heidi*

Dear Ring-Ring!-It's-for-Heidi:

Yes, it sounds like your cat is under a lot of pressure and a possible candidate for a nervous breakdown. I can picture him lying on that special cat psychiatric couch, his little head on the doily, crumpled tissues on the floor, as he tells Dr. Dumpling about his troubled kittyhood. Heidi, get a grip. If you believe that Sir Cat has any feelings about, let alone gets depressed, every time you use your gold card, I have a tooth fairy that I'd like to introduce you to. In fact, recent experiments by the Department of Agriculture proved that blindfolded test cats were unable to differentiate between a glamorous celebrity owner who lives in the Trump Towers and a less fortunate owner who had just four teeth and lived in an empty kitchen appliance box.

P.S. If you still feel guilty, buy a tiny designer parachute and take him skydiving, or, if he's not keen on heights, take him to your Pilates class.

# A CAT LOVER'S PLEDGE

I will not reduce my standards and settle for just any old cat (unless it's soooooooooooooooo cute).

I will not be with a cat who works off excess energy by taunting the dog.

I will not be with a cat who doesn't rush over and drape itself across my shoulders when I feel a draft.

I will not "forgive" a cat who turns my cashmere sweater into a pot holder.

I will not be with a cat who shamelessly flirts with everyone but me.

I will not be with a cat who isn't sure she wants to be with me.

I will not be with a cat who doesn't demonstrably worship me.

I will not be with a cat who's a no-show for our play date.

I will not be with a cat who responds to my come-hither look by pretending to be cross-eyed.

I will not be with a cat who's afraid to talk about our future.

I will not be with a cat who acts like she "loves it when I hold her," then jumps 500 feet in the air if she hears a noise.

I will not be with a cat who's too self-absorbed to appreciate when I wear my "Cats Are the Best" T-shirt.

I will not be with a pre-owned cat who treats me just like her last owner.

I will not be with a cat who can't behave herself at a sushi bar.

**FULL DISCLOSURE NOTE:** *To better identify with the 85,000,000 cat owners in the U.S., simply remove the word "not" from the above sentences.*

# How Many Cats Per Person?

Rule of thumb for those who don't mind the fact that cats are just not that into them.

| IF YOU'RE A . . . | SUGGESTED NUMBER OF CATS |
|---|---|
| Woman living in a small apartment, not lonely but loves animals, hates walking a dog. | 1–2 |
| Woman living in a huge apartment, very lonely but Match.com isn't working for you. | 40 |
| Retired couple, children seldom call, still wrestling with empty-nest syndrome. Need a pet to love but HMO doesn't cover allergy to parakeets. | 3 |
| Elderly woman not quite right in the head, wears tinfoil hat, certain that the CIA is out to get her. | 29 |
| Newly divorced male, shell-shocked, need companionship but women you've been dating smell the loneliness. | 12 |
| Confirmed cat lover, tad psychotic, fond of strays, especially those transfixed by your lava lamp. | 9 |
| Late-fifties bachelor, still lives with mother. Want reliable nonhuman source of affection who won't constantly tell you to sit up straight. | 14 |
| Woman, insecure about your looks. When you ask, "Do these shoes go with my outfit?" need second, third, fourth, fifth, and sixth opinion. | 6 |
| Prisoner, in for larceny, theft, grand theft, murder, and jaywalking, seeking nonjudgmental cell-mate for cramped cell. | 1 |

# THE "MAYBE SHE NEEDS HER OWN SPACE" EXCUSE

Dear Richard:

My cat, Muffin, is a warm, wonderful creature. But only part-time. One moment she's purring in my lap, smiling at me (I think), then off she goes the next minute, disappearing for hours, sometimes for days, and doing heaven knows what. I know certain cats are independent and have huge libidos, and I'm pretty sure she thinks about me a lot when she's gone. Right? I can trust her, right? Should I trust her?

*Greg*

P.S. She's recently begun shaving her legs.

Dear I Seek to Understand the Mystery of the Disappearing Cat:

Even with a good pitching arm, trust her only as far as you can throw her. You want a "faithful" cat? Now hear this: Your cat is "into you" when she sees you, and even then only if you meet her halfway by kneeling. The rest of the time her mind's on other stream-of-consciousness things—mice, birds, sex, and Elton John. Let the following rule of thumb be your guide. Never trust a cat who:

· Brings up stuff that happened months ago.

· At one year of age is still "getting her life together."

· Puts you on hold while she grooms herself.

· Before going out, places a dab of Shalimar behind each ear.

· You met in detox.

# THE "MAYBE SHE DIDN'T RECOGNIZE ME IN MY NEW HAWAIIAN SHIRT" EXCUSE

Dear Richard:

    I'm devastated. Last weekend, while visiting my next-door neighbor, I had a brief fling with her cat, Sonja, a really cute Manx. She rubbed against my leg, purred, and played enthusiastically with the twine I was dangling. Then, yesterday, I went over there again and that very same cat *acted as if she didn't know me!* As though I didn't exist! Am I hurt? Well, duh! Was I a passing fancy? Does she think she can just use me, then toss me away like an empty sardine can? And, yet, something tells me it's nothing more than a tactic to seduce me.

    Sobbing in Omaha,

*Calvin*

Dear Overworked Tear Ducts:

    Hello! The cat wasn't being insensitive, it's just that the portion of the cat's brain that controls attachment to humans is only slightly smaller than that of a helium atom. You, my friend, sound like a real catch, especially if you have your own twine, and you deserve a cat of your own, a demonstrative one who worships and adores you. Where are these particular cats found? As of this writing, on some yet undiscovered planet. If you find one, I'll buy it from you for $750,000, cash.

## NEEDINESS ALERT

# ARE YOU IN DANGER OF YOUR CAT BEING INTO YOU?

You do all the right things—you're familiar but not friendly, you let her sleep on your bed but get appropriately testy if she sheds, you use the everyday china for her bowl, you lavish extra love and attention only on her birthday and Valentine's Day, you clean the yecch from the corners of her eyes only when she walks into walls, and if she's been extra naughty, you are not above closing the hide-a-bed with her still in it.

Yet the signs are there. She loves your lap. She follows you around the house. She's ecstatic when you pet her and she melts when you read her *Puss 'n Boots*. She watches you sleep and meows extra softly when you're hungover. Does this mean that she's gradually getting into you?

In your dreams.

# HOLIDAYS APPROACHING?

## GIFTS FOR THE CAT WHO HAS EVERYTHING

*1.* Does she have her own yoga mat?

*2.* Wouldn't she rather watch *Tom & Jerry* on a *flat screen* TV?

*3.* How about her very own boneless turkey breast, instead of making her grovel for a portion of yours?

*4.* For the ultra-clean kitty: an après-kitty litter bidet.

*5.* Have you considered melting her heart with a dazzling but tasteful tiny diamond tennis bracelet for her right front paw? (If you're broke, a wrist corsage is acceptable.)

*6.* How about a menorah made out of salt cod?

Not to worry: Between Thanksgiving and Christmas, most cats, especially those partial to fruitcake and turkey giblets, put on a few extra pounds. Be certain your cat makes dieting a part of her New Year's resolutions.

# Test Your Cat I.Q. (Advanced)

After studying the 25 adjectives below, decide which best apply to an owner and which best apply to his or her cat.

| ADJECTIVE | OWNER | CAT |
|---|---|---|
| *1.* Indulgent | | |
| *2.* Doting | | |
| *3.* Servile | | |
| *4.* Obedient | | |
| *5.* Humble | | |
| *6.* Meek | | |
| *7.* Insecure | | |
| *8.* Neurotic | | |
| *9.* Dependent | | |
| *10.* Codependent | | |
| *11.* Autocratic | | |
| *12.* Intelligent | | |
| *13.* Needy | | |
| *14.* Tolerant | | |
| *15.* Easily manipulated by to-die-for cute cat[1] | | |
| *16.* Fears rejection | | |
| *17.* Fickle | | |
| *18.* Passive | | |
| *19.* Passive-aggressive | | |
| *20.* Dictatorial | | |
| *21.* Submissive | | |
| *22.* Dignified | | |
| *23.* Noble | | |
| *24.* Loving | | |
| *25.* Unconditionally loving | | |

[1]*Okay, it's a phrase, sue me.*

# Answers

| ADJECTIVE | OWNER | CAT |
|---|---|---|
| *1.* Indulgent | X | |
| *2.* Doting | X | |
| *3.* Servile | X | |
| *4.* Obedient | X | |
| *5.* Humble | X | |
| *6.* Meek | X | |
| *7.* Insecure | X | |
| *8.* Neurotic | X | |
| *9.* Dependent | X | |
| *10.* Codependent | X | |
| *11.* Autocratic | | X |
| *12.* Intelligent | | X |
| *13.* Needy | X | |
| *14.* Tolerant | X | |
| *15.* Easily manipulated by to-die-for cute cat | (guess) | |
| *16.* Fears rejection | X | |
| *17.* Fickle | | X |
| *18.* Passive | X | |
| *19.* Passive-aggressive | | X |
| *20.* Dictatorial | | X |
| *21.* Submissive | X | |
| *22.* Dignified | | X |
| *23.* Noble | | X |
| *24.* Loving | X | X |
| *25.* Unconditionally loving | X | |

NOTE: It took cat fancier Mabel Beak of Clancy, Alabama, just three months to score a perfect 25. How did you do?

## Chapter Five

YOUR CAT'S JUST *NOT* THAT INTO YOU . . .

# If He's Emotionally Unavailable

*Could it be, dear owner, that you're
looking for love in all the wrong places?*

Of course you want more from your cat. And you make all kinds of excuses: I'm not her type. My cat is scared of intimacy. She's afraid of rejection if she makes a first move and puts her paw around me. Or her parents split up when she was just a kitty and now she has trouble "trusting." Don't you wish your cat would drop her guard for just a few moments? Of course you do! Well, stop. Just stop. It's not going to happen. How do I know? After two years and $11,000 worth of therapy with a leading cat psychologist, my previous cat, Benrus, still drew the blinds when he used the litter box.

# THE "SHE'D LOVE ME IF SHE KNEW THE REAL ME" EXCUSE

Dear Richard:

I've noticed that with inanimate objects—mops, a pile of sweaters, Grandpa—my Juliet has no intimacy issues. With me, she's always playful, practically purrs on command, has thick, gorgeous fur and best of all, her color matches my eyes. Yet she doesn't like to be physically affectionate. She runs away whenever I try to pick her up. Is it just that she needs to get to know me better? Do you think she comes from a dysfunctional family?

*Irena*

Dear Right, Her Mommy Didn't Touch Her Enough:
How does she feel about washcloths? Sponges? I say give her time. Many cats hide their emotions because, as kittens, they felt repressed, especially if they had to share their mom with another kitten (see *Sibling Rivalry in Siamese* by Horst Bibble). They need a lot of time to heal and trust. However, if after a year it's still just a platonic relationship, buy an affectionate bat.

# THE "MAYBE SHE HAS A DRESS CODE" EXCUSE

Dear Richard:

Ginger, my three-year-old Himalayan, loves to chew on my underwear, except when I'm wearing them. No matter how much I invite her to go "bite-bite" and give her the run of my panties, she'll savor them only if they're lying on the floor or on the bed. Do you think she just respects me too much to feast on my undies when I'm wearing them?

*Elaine*

Dear In Search of a Cheap Thrill:

Call it what you want, cats love to use those pretty little teeth. What they find mouth-watering is totally unpredictable. Jar of open peanut butter mysteriously half-empty? Does Mr. Fur Ball look guilty? Toupee missing? Kitty suddenly emerges from a stuffed turkey with a guilty look? Guess who the culprit is. Elaine, this is just a hunch, but you could try to get Ginger to be more into you by wearing something slinky, like a black satin negligee.

# THE "ZING WENT THE STRINGS OF MY HEART" EXCUSE

Dear Richard:

   After reading of the health benefits of owning a cat (I have an impacted wisdom tooth, plus I'm neurotic), but being on a tight budget, I was delighted when my local pet store sold me Elsie at a discount because she was a floor sample. After checking her out, I decided she was just as good, if not better, than a full-priced cat, plus the owner threw in a set of steak knives. At first, I had high expectations. I fell in love with this warm, furry creature who was affectionate and loving. When I sat down, she'd scamper over and jump on my lap, we always cuddled in bed, and on many nights I'd happily fall asleep to her purring. Sometimes, if she got up early enough, we'd have breakfast together before I left for work. I was really starting to feel healthy. Now, all of a sudden, she's just not that into me. When I try to make a play date with her, she yawns and walks away. If I try to snuggle, she emits a tepid meow. She rejected the heart-shaped cat cookies I baked that beat even when reheated. Do you think Elsie has a past that she's not telling me about?

*Noreen*

Dear The Honeymoon Is Over:

Will Elsie come to her senses? Will Noreen realize that she has to get better on her own because her cat no longer makes house calls? Tune in next time for another episode of that new reality show "Naive Cat Owner for a Day." Look, Noreen, unlike simple beasts, like a mule or a surfer, cats are complicated and mercurial. One minute they're loving you to pieces; a few seconds later they're plundering your rose garden while singing, "I Got You, Babe." Do they care about your health? Do they know anything about HMOs? Do they know that a paper cut can make you cry? Whether your cat is a pedigree or one of Omaha's One Hundred Neediest Cat Cases, love at first sight applies only to its owner. Your basic off-the-rack cat cares only that it's warm, snug, fed, and, at least once a month, getting it on with someone their own size.

## REJECTION ADVISORIES TO ALL CAT OWNERS

1. A cat who, when peeved or cranky, says, "You're not my real owner," still may be involved with her last owner.

2. Your cat doesn't care that you use his photo as your screen saver.

3. A bust of your cat on the mantle is no guarantee that she'll be into you.

# THE "MAYBE SHE NEEDS SOME TIME ALONE" EXCUSE

Dear Richard:

    Lately my cat, Madonna, has been really weird. To begin with, she's purring in a different key, her kisses are less ardent (even if I make the first move), and yesterday she responded to my "come-hither" look by coughing up some bile. And she's been very fussy. Her usual green feeding dish suddenly isn't good enough; it has to be the blue one decorated with tiny canaries. To make matters worse, her once-gentle love bites are leaving exit wounds. We've been together for three years and I really love her. I keep telling myself Madonna really still loves me, too, but is going through a "phase." Wait, Richard, I know what you're going to say, but I'm pretty sure she's not seeing someone else. I'm sure Madonna will go back to her old loving self if I'm patient, right?

*Clyde*

Dear You've Been Snoozing in Class Again:

Madonna is exhibiting all the signs of the three-year itch, in which cats, after a "honeymoon" period, are tempted to seek romance outside the owner–cat relationship. Ask yourself:

• Would Madonna rather stare into a mouse hole than your eyes?

• Does she no longer get misty-eyed when you watch *When Harry Met Sally* together?

• Does she suddenly think lying in bed reading the Sunday paper is "corny"?

• Is she sleeping on the laundry instead of helping you fold it?

• Was that her face you saw on match.com?

## EXTRA-HELPFUL AFFECTION ADVISORY!

Cats adore the owner who can't keep his hands off his cat. It makes kitty feel loved, wanted, needed, sexy, serene, and best of all, totally in control of her owner.

Look, Clyde, I'm sorry you feel unloved, but a cat's wonder-lust is exceeded only by its wanderlust—rare is the cat who doesn't occasionally crave a moonlit stroll or a tryst with someone equally furry. Your cat is not a crutch. Look for unconditional love elsewhere—a gerbil who's in mourning or a needy frog.

# THE "MAYBE THE LIGHTING WAS BAD" EXCUSE

Dear Richard:

I'm crushed. Last week, after months of sitting home alone watching TV, and after rearranging my collection of cold pizza slices, I had this amazing blind date. We flirted, I made her laugh, we discovered we had tons in common, and best of all, I could tell she was really into me. I began to feel kind of close, so I pulled out my wallet and showed her several photos of Groucho, my beloved American Shorthair, in various and adorable poses, including one of him wearing his little clown  hat and another (my favorite) of his tongue in the toaster. Guess what: Not only did she not gush, she snapped her fingers and ordered a large glass of gin. Suddenly, everything cooled. After taking her home, when I asked whether I might see her again, she said she had recently joined the Peace Corps and would be spending the next twelve years in the Republic of Cameroon. What should I do?

*Todd*

Dear You're So Much Better Off
Without Her In Your Life:

Girlfriends come and go, but a cat who wears a clown hat? It's a no-brainer, Todd—go with that feeling of loneliness. Cat love is better and much more reliable than human love. Have you ever heard of a cat withholding sex because you forgot her anniversary? Do you ever come home tired and weary and then have to listen to your cat tell you about his day? On a Saturday morning, has Groucho ever told you that instead of playing golf, you have to go to your AA meeting? With Groucho, at least you know where you stand: You *know* he's not that into you, and best of all, you never have to worry that Groucho will run off with your best friend.

P.S. If you're worried she might change her mind, send her a photo of Groucho with a little note saying, "I'm giving you one more chance." I'm sure it'll work.

You want kitty to show how much she loves you, assuming she knows who you are. But cats have their own ways of being demonstrative, none of which involve actual affection. Remember: There are no bad cats, only insufficiently submissive owners.

## THE "SHE'S JUST TRYING TO FIND HERSELF" EXCUSE

Dear Richard:

My cat, Buttons, is sweet and wonderful and I know we're emotionally involved. But most of the time, instead of making me feel like the center of her universe (is that asking so much? I do, after all, feed, care for, and love her), she spends much of her free "quality" time chasing her tail and running up and down the stairs, often for hours. I don't understand why she doesn't get bored or at least throw up from spinning and running so much. It occurs to me that she's either seeking her inner child or may think she's churning butter (she's a former farm cat). Do you think she needs a sedative?

*Dennis*

### TWO SUPER-IMPORTANT CAT TIPS

*1.* If a black cat crosses your path either:

- Buy a lottery ticket
- Use a different hiking trail

*2.* Uttering, "Wow, you're so beautiful, I can't believe that you're not owned," means you're about to bring home your 14th stray.

Dear Unable to Recognize the Difference Between Horse Power and Cat Power:

Okay, Dennis, let's talk about Buttons. She's having a great time being a cat. Does she know it's her tail she's chasing? Does she know that chasing a long, furry thing is the classic manifestation of what Dr. Laura calls "tail envy"? That while she's being a whirling dervish you're pining for her attention? Probably not. Do you know why? Bingo! Because she's just not that into you. True, the occasional frustration of being the owner of a not-fully-into-you cat can make even the sanest owner occasionally reach for a Klonopin the size of a mah-jongg tile. But be tolerant, you must let your cat be herself. Instead of stuffing yourself with drugs, would you consider seeing a grief counselor? (Individual results may vary.)

Sorry you're feeling rejected, but the operative word here is entitlement. Without it, a cat would be either Mother Teresa or a bad prom date. Go easy on yourself. Stop fantasizing about that "ideal" cat who comes when called, stands on its hind legs, begs for scraps, and experiences chest pains when it sees you having a better time playing with the dog.

# Quiz: Know Thy Kitty

1. **Which of the following cat breeds is *least* likely to be into you:**

   *a.* Ragdoll

   *b.* Norwegian Forest

   *c.* Scottish Fold

   *d.* Siamese

   *e.* Maine Coon

   *f.* Turkish Angora

   *g.* Manx

   *h.* American Shorthair

2. **TRUE OR FALSE:** Even if she's not that into you, cuddling with your warm, comforting, lovable cat can replace 96 percent of the bodily fluids lost when your brother-in-law wants to borrow money.

## Chapter Six

Your Cat's Just *Not* That Into You . . .

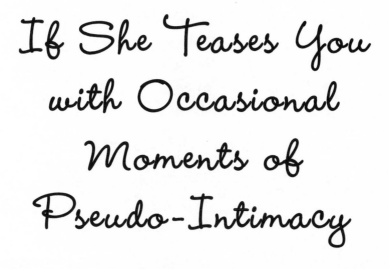

# If She Teases You with Occasional Moments of Pseudo-Intimacy

*If a cat is really into you, she's not afraid to talk about "our future."*

Okay, even though she made the first move, your cat scratched your tongue when you tried to strum her whiskers. Your excuse? She's not quite ready for that degree of intimacy. I know it's hard. You love your cat unconditionally (there's that U-word again) and you want her to love you back. Well, she does, but in her own way. (See J. J. Gittle's monograph, "Resistance and Repression in Alley Cats.") Once you accept this, you're on your way to cat owner paradise, that place where well-adjusted owners are grateful for any crumbs of affection kitty deigns to give. Oh, and P.S. to Dee Dee in Vermont: Your cat, Olio, is meowing someone else's name in her sleep? Did it ever occur to you it's only because, for a cat, especially with so tiny a tongue, Dee Dee is a hard name to pronounce? Think about it.

## THE "YOU THINK IT'S AFFECTION, WHEREAS YOUR CAT MERELY THINKS YOU'RE DELICIOUS" EXCUSE

Dear Richard:

Lately, when my Scottish Fold, Algebra, licks my face, her tongue feels unusually dry. It makes me feel less loved. Usually her tongue is dripping wet. Does she need more liquid?

*April*

Dear April Showers:

Good news. The connection between a cat's love and salivary state when she licks you was first observed in 1963 by Sir Hiram Pilsner, whose "Wetness Classification Table" is now considered the gold standard of how much a cat is into you.

### The Pilsner Face-Lick Wetness Scale

(0 = Not into you. 100 = Most into you.)

| Moisture Factor | How Into You Kitty Is |
| --- | --- |
| Drought (tongue like sandpaper) | .00000000002 |
| Damp (you feel a little love, but not nearly enough to satisfy) | .000000007 |
| Wet (that's more like it) | .000000015 |
| Very wet (eyes misting up—yours) | .000000023 |
| Soaked (reminds you of first husband) | .000000031 |
| Drenched (wondering if things are getting out of hand) | .000000037 |
| Saturated (toying with idea of telling kitty to "snap out of it," but it feels too good) | .000000043 |
| Standing in a puddle | .00000164 |

# THE "CAN'T WE STILL BE FRIENDS?" EXCUSE

Dear Richard:

    I used to think I was the love of my cat's life, but now I feel starved for Zeitgeist's affection. The moment I used to get home, we'd get all cozy on the sofa, intertwine our limbs, and watch Fox News. Lately, however, she's been, well, distant. She doesn't smile at me, she doesn't wear the little scarf I got her, and when I hold her, she licks my face only four times, down from a high of 36. Is the honeymoon over, or is she suddenly repressing her love for me by reliving some weird kittyhood trauma? Maybe she was frightened by thunder? Or is it possible that she's one of those cats with intimacy issues?

*Serena*

Dear Dr. Ruth:

Yeah, that's it. Thunder. Or she's a psychological mess because when she was a kitten she got no answer to her letter to Santa. News flash: Cats are fickle and unpredictable. I knew a cat who always sat on her owner's lap when he was on the toilet. Then, all of a sudden, the cat found God and her owner died of constipation. You have a choice: Accept the truth and settle for an unrequited relationship, or make her jealous by getting a handsome teddy bear and make an extravagant show of loving it ... and settle for an unrequited relationship.

Cats do love to sleep with their owner, and according to an informal poll, the softer the bed linen (300 thread count minimum), the deeper the cat's sleep. When a cat is ready to wake up and start its day, however, it doesn't worry about disturbing its still-snoozing owner, or whether its departure will interrupt a hot dream. Cats are just not into that.

# EXACTLY HOW NOT INTO YOU IS YOUR CAT?
## Official Scale of Feline Indifference

Explanation: .00000000000000001 = least into you; 1 = totally into you)

| ACTIVITY | DEGREE OF INTO-YOU-NESS |
|---|---|
| Doesn't play with new toy purchased with hard-earned babysitting money. Instead, it's at the bottom of her toy pile. | .000000001 |
| Lovingly bites your toes to restore circulation after you've been shoveling snow for two hours. | .01 |
| Scampers away when you try to get a group shot for the family Christmas photo. | .0001 |
| Looks puzzled when you hold her up, and in your best ventriloquist kitty-voice (key of A-flat), pretend she's talking to your boyfriend, but goes with it, anyway. | .01 |
| Drops a decomposing mouse before you as you're dry-heaving from tainted potato salad. | .0000000001 |
| Yawns and starts grooming herself when you ask, "Should I go for a grunge look?" | .00000001 |
| Vigorously nods her head up and down when you ask, "Do these jeans make me look fat?" | .00001 |
| You find her in the bedroom playing with your best toupee. | .0001 |
| Pees on it when you leave a burning cigarette in the ashtray. | .01 |
| Flirts with pizza delivery man. | .000001 |

| ACTIVITY | DEGREE OF INTO-YOU-NESS |
|---|---|
| Exhibits not one morsel of "Please don't leave me" fear of abandonment when you leave for work. | .00001 |
| Her little heart beats only a trifle faster when you gently blow in her ear. | .001 |
| Doesn't blush when she uses the kitty litter in front of company. | .00001 |
| Eats your homework. | .000000000000001 |
| Sits beside you so you can ride in the HOV lane. (Note: You lose .01 if she keeps asking, "Are we there yet?") | .1 |

## Advisory to Elizabeth

"If only my cat knew what I went through to get him?" Pay attention, Liz, I'm here to help. Just because you wanted Rugby, your pedigreed Himalayan, so badly that you bought him with a stolen credit card does not mean he is yours or will do your bidding, any more than a cat bought with cash or a valid check. Cats don't really know or care how they were acquired and can't grasp the concept of "My owner risked a stretch in the pen for me, so I will be a good and obedient cat." On the other hand, "foundling" cats, left on a doorstep with a little note saying, "Please give me a good home, my old one sucked," can be a different story.

# THE "SHOULD I TAKE THE HINT AND SHAVE MY LEGS?" EXCUSE

Dear Richard:

Here's the problem: Jonquil, my Burmese, used to love to rub against my legs—so much so that, to provide easier access, I started wearing a kilt. When I'd get home, she'd positively relish my legs, even giving me whisker burns. Lately, however, she's dumped me for a table leg. I'm mystified. I'm thinking, maybe if I shave my legs, or coat them with anchovy paste, I'll regain the pleasure of my furry feline. Do you think she's no longer that into me?

*Quigley*

Hey, Mr. Wondering What Your Cat Has Against You: Ain't working with an inarticulate cat a bitch? Another example of cat owners straining their brains, wondering, "How can I make myself more attractive, more indispensable to my cat? What's so hard about worshipping me?" Sorry, pal, your cat is going through the classic I-prefer-furniture phase and there's nothing you can do about it. Will she "love" you again? Probably. Will she molest your legs again? Have no fear; she'll do so in her own good time.

# Quiz: Know Thy Kitty

You and your cat are sitting on the sofa, watching your favorite movie (*Casablanca*) and sharing a box of popcorn. Suddenly, she pulls her sweet, little paw from your hand, emits a hasty growl, and disappears into the next room. Do you:

*a.* Assume she got antsy and mutter, "Cats will be cats."

*b.* Hit the hold button on your DVD player, and reach for another handful of popcorn.

*c.* Wait for her to return, no matter how long it takes.

*d.* Assume she's no longer a fan of Peter Lorre.

*e.* Realize your cat's just not that into you and get a better cat.

*f.* Call out to her to please bring you another Diet Pepsi.

Bravo! You answered *a.* Aren't you happy you made the right choice? (Note: If you chose *e*, go with it. You're wonderful and deserve to be with your soulmate. He's out there—just be patient and don't settle.)

*Advisory to P.M.S. in Duluth*

I'm glad you asked, although I suspect you're not going to be thrilled with my answer. The percentage of the average cat's brain devoted to how he or she can be more that into their wonderful, devoted, caring, giving, one-in-a-million owner is .0000000000000000000003 percent.

## THE "MAYBE IF I HAD DESIGNER SHEETS?" EXCUSE

Dear Richard:

It was one of those perfect mornings. There I was, lying in bed with my cuddly Maine Coon, Shakespeare, snuggled up against me, his eyes half-closed, purring and exuding warmth like a giant, smelly heating pad. All was serene until suddenly he meowed, and in a matter of seconds was off the bed and in the next room. I didn't understand. I was still as a mouse, stroking his fur, and simply enjoying his presence. Did I do something wrong? Should I have let him get under the quilt? I really thought Shakespeare and I were having a "moment."

*Allie*

Dear Perhaps He Went to Fetch Your Coffee?:

Are you (still) lying down? Good, then I can tell you that, with cats, that's all there is—a moment, which pretty much sums up their attention span. Shakespeare wasn't with you one moment and gone the next; he was gone even while he was there, much like some men who, during a night of bliss, seem to have already put on their clothes and left. The difference, of course, is that cats don't have clothes to put on. Also, they don't even think, "Should I promise to call?" Cats prefer to focus on their real ambitions, which are to a) not have any ambition and b) torment their owners with what cat psychologist Mandrake Kline terms their Reverse Vibrissa Response.

Do you not get it? How many more pages will it take? Cats live according to their own rules and regulations! They have no time for being into you, let alone *that* into you! Lower your expectations! You have nothing to lose but your delusions! Rare is the cat who, if not in the mood, will come when called, sit quietly in your lap, or help you in a bar fight.

# THE SCHNAPPS-PORSCHE WELL-ADJUSTED CAT OWNER ANALYSIS

NOTE: THERE ARE NO WRONG ANSWERS, JUST SAD ONES.

### 1) When did you realize you were not the center of your cat's universe?

☐ *From day one. (I should have known. She was a foundling from the Home Shopping Network.)*

☐ *Last night, when she refused to spoon with me.*

☐ *When she came home pregnant.*

☐ *When she came home wearing a tongue stud.*

### 2) How do you react when your cat does something that really irritates you?

☐ *Fly into a rage.*

☐ *Lie down in a fetal position and hold my breath until she shapes up.*

☐ *You're exhilarated—she's her own little person!*

### 3) Which statement best applies to your cat?

☐ *Furry and snuggly.*

☐ *Sleek and proud.*

☐ *His incessant and tuneless meowing is starting to get to me.*

### 4) You keep a photo of your cat:

☐ *On your desk.*

☐ *On the refrigerator.*

☐ *In the refrigerator.*

### 5) Which clinical condition best typifies the relation between you and kitty?

☐ *A tad obsessive.*

☐ *Cat-dependent.*

☐ *Discreet soul kisses.*

## Chapter Seven

YOUR CAT'S JUST *NOT* THAT INTO YOU . . .

# If She Toys with Your Self-Esteem

*You shouldn't have to devote several therapy sessions to discussing how insecure your cat makes you feel, especially when you see her cuddling with a mop.*

"I don't understand," began one letter from an upset owner who had just seen her cat's face on singlejews.com, "I always go for emotionally unavailable cats." Oh, sure, your cat loves and needs you!—but on her terms. Who doesn't want a cat who emits a warm meow when you get home, or with a knowing nod, lets you know how great you look in those new spring capri pants. Does this cat exist? No. Do cats consider their owners mere chattel? This was demonstrated in the famous Prague Experiment of 1949, when a cat was placed in a room and asked to choose among five different men. Did the cat choose its owner? Hardly. It went straight for the one person in the room wearing brushed corduroy slacks.

## THE "ANIMAL MAGNETISM VS. HUMAN MAGNETISM" EXCUSE

Dear Richard:

Help! My cats aren't in love with my new boyfriend. I finally met the man of my dreams—he's so totally into me—but my twin cats, Bell and Belfry, don't like him. The minute Scott comes over, they gang up and attack him, clawing his arms, staring daggers if he playfully snaps my thong, meowing at the top of their lungs if we play music and dance, and (this is so embarrassing) when we have an intimate, candlelit dinner, the cats jump up on the table and blow out the candles. Scott, on the other hand, goes out of his way to be nice. He brings them toys, he invites them to sit on his lap and shed to their hearts' content, but they just sniff and scamper away to some distant corner of the house to plot their next anti-Scott strategy. I adore Scott and I love my beautiful kitties to death. What's a woman to do?

*Daphne*

Well, Boo Hoo, Daphne:

When it comes to animal magnetism vs. human magnetism, guess who's going to win? Life is hard enough without getting involved with someone whom your cats appear to loathe. (Notice the "whom"; cats are impressed by good grammar.) Your poor boyfriend is being victimized by two little cats? Get over it. Boyfriends come and go, but really great cats are hard to find. You deserve to be with someone whom your cats really dig. The next time you visit a singles bar, you'll save yourself much grief if you bring your cats along, and let them decide who buys you a drink.

**Note:** Daphne? Listen to me. If you're truly hung up on Scott, try this: Show your cats who's in charge by visiting your local pet store and buying a Deluxe Siegfried and Roy Mini-Taming Kit for Cats. For just $29.95, you get a pith helmet, a tiny chair, and a junior whip.

# THE "IT'S ALL MY FAULT" EXCUSE

Dear Richard:

The other day, while grooming herself, Hortense, my beautiful and golden-coated tabby (she recently won Most Luscious Cat in a Getty station contest), noticed she had a ton of split ends. She seems to think that I'm responsible. I understand that cats are particular about their appearance, especially in harsh light, and I want to be there for her, but how can I explain to her that I had nothing to do with it? Should I take her to a groomer who can convince her?

*Karen*

Yes, Karen, It's All Your Fault:

When it's humid, does kitty blame you for her frizzies? If it's a cloudy day, does she make you stand in the corner because there's no sun for her to bask in? Does she scold you if you're one minute late feeding her because your water broke? This is just one of the things that makes cats so fascinating. However, the next time this happens, spray her with the garden hose. Then she'll at least have something to blame you for.

## STRAIGHT FROM THE KITTY LITTER

Friends don't let friends talk baby talk to their cat:

1. When out in public
2. During a job interview
3. When their date arrives to pick them up
4. In front of other cats
5. At their class reunion

Because it . . .

a) does not make your cat more that into you and

b) irritates the cat who wants to feel grown-up (discreetly blowing kisses at your cat from across the room is okay)

To feel in control, cat owners make all kinds of excuses for their cats. "She'd be ever so demonstrative if only she allowed herself to show her true feelings." "He's sending me perfervid messages of love—it's just that they're so subtle that I, a mere human, can't pick them up." "She's overjoyed to see me when I get home, turning her back is just her way of showing it." "A truly evolved cat would consider napping between my bare thighs a religious experience." You must keep telling yourself this, since the truth is too much to bear.

ARE YOU POWERLESS OVER YOUR CAT?

# WARNING SIGNS THAT YOU'RE READY FOR THE CAT LOVERS ANONYMOUS 12-STEP PROGRAM

1. You have wall-to-wall carpeting in your cat carrier.

2. You have 43 or more books with the word "cat" in their title.

3. You have a wall calendar featuring cats.

4. You live alone in a cheap apartment with 62 strays and a can opener.

5. You never go on vacation because your cat might get "lonely," even though she would have no idea that you're gone.

6. You once ate cat food allegedly to see how it tastes, but really to be "at one" with your cat.

7. So she'd feel included, you had an ice sculpture of your cat at your wedding.

> **BONUS WARNING SIGNS**
>
> - After making her promise to be quiet, have you ever smuggled your cat into a movie?
> - For her birthday, did you take her in a hansom cab through Central Park?
> - How often do you give her a piggyback ride?

8. You're convinced the presence of your cat would have made the honeymoon more memorable.

9. You have a special thermometer that determines if kitty's food is the precise temperature at which Miss Fussy likes it.

10. During your last poker game, you kept your cat on your lap "for good luck."

11. You have no problem with the fact that she grooms herself with your tongue.

# Quiz: Know Thy Kitty

**1. A group of cats is called:**

   *a.* A squadron

   *b.* A gaggle

   *c.* A clowder

   *d.* A jazz quartet

   *e.* The Hadassah

**2. Which of the following especially-not-that-into-you cat breeds *does* exist:**

   *a.* Himalayan Cha-Cha

   *b.* Bengal Vonce

   *c.* Egyptian Mau

   *d.* Nascar Mullet

   *e.* Slim Jim

   *f.* Narragansett Pacer

ANSWERS: 1. You answered C? Very good. (Unless you're one of those cat hoarders who has 22 cats roaming your one-bedroom apartment. Then the correct answer is A.) 2. If you answered C again, you really know your cats. (Although B is currently seeking accreditation from a Tel Aviv cat club.)

## *Advisory to Olivia*

Many thanks for the photo of Rumps, your three-year-old Abyssinian. Indeed she's cute. Unfortunately, I have a policy against publishing photos, candid or otherwise, of any cat with a wedgie.

# THE "I THOUGHT HE WAS TRYING TO SHAPE UP FOR BATHING SUIT SEASON" EXCUSE

Dear Richard:

Ever heard the expression "Fat Cat"? Well that's Orson, my fabulous Persian. Yes, he's chubby and self-conscious about his double chin, but I love him for his mind *and* his body. Lately, though, he's been eating less and exercising more. The other day, in the laundry room, I caught him doing ab crunches, and when I'm on the treadmill, he shoves me aside, hops on, and tries to get his heart rate up. He even bought himself new miniature Adidas. At first I thought he just wanted to shape up for bathing suit season (who doesn't?), but could it be something more sinister? A new relationship? Do you think he's sleeping with someone else? Someone he wants to impress? I thought I was being overly suspicious until I discovered this chart, pasted to the wall in an unused part of our basement:

# CALORIE CHART FOR WEIGHT-WATCHING CATS

| ACTIVITY | CALORIES BURNED (per 10 minutes) |
|---|---|
| Squash: | |
| *Cat against cat* | 34 |
| *Cat against human.* | 7 |
| Light Housework: | |
| *Helping owner fold pile of laundry* | 22 |
| *Dozing on it* | 3 |
| Moderate Housework: | |
| *Mopping floor with tail* | 31 |
| *Jumping rope* | 44 |
| *Jumping string* | 20 |
| *Listening to the radio* | 6 |
| *Plotting against dog* | 19 |
| Heavy housework: | |
| *Ironing* | 17 |
| *Riding on iron while owner moves it back and forth* | 4 |
| Licking fur: | |
| *Using own tongue* | 55 |
| *Using hamster's tongue* | 100 |
| Purring: | |
| *Real* | 22 |
| *Faked* | 50 |
| Flirting: | |
| *With pizza delivery person* | 10 |
| *With comely mouse* | 2 |
| Kissing owner: | |
| *Puckering up* | 8 |
| *Carpentry* | 15 |

Am I being paranoid, or what?

*Katerina*

Dear Other Woman:

I feel your pain.

I suggest looking for further "weight shedding" clues. Is your cat chewing his food more slowly? Refusing seconds? Has he asked for a smaller bowl so his portions look larger? Is he substituting water for his usual hot dogs? And—this is the real test—does he shower the moment he gets home? No matter how often you've just answered "yes," don't interfere. If you give him time, maybe he'll realize what a fabulous and wonderful person you are, stop cheating, and come back to you. If not, change the locks.

Cat owners tend to overestimate their pets' capabilities. Are there genuinely talented cats? Yes. Certain breeds, if given enough brandy, can be trained to slide over their owner's back and render a pretty fair shiatsu massage. Born-again cats suddenly develop a fondness for Christian rock. Others, like insomniac cats, can be taught to drink heavily.

# THE "THESE PAWS ARE MADE FOR WALKIN'" EXCUSE

Dear Richard:

Whenever I'm sitting at the computer, my cat, Balzac, likes to jump up and walk on the keyboard. She seems fascinated by the keys—sometimes I even take her sweet little front paws and try to teach her to "type" her name. If I leave her alone, however, she carefully places her right paw on the "Delete" key and taps it several times. Is she just being playful or is this her way of telling me that the screenplay I'm writing (*Tails of Two Kitties*) is junk?

*Adolfus*

Dear Only If She's Hitting the Delete Key with Claw Extended:

How fun! You have your own little editor. Look, my friend, without attracting the wrath of the social services branch of PETA, may I suggest that a) a cat's communication skills do not include the ability to distinguish letters—he could just as well be tapping the "Backspace" key and b) think more of yourself—the title sounds promising.

# THE "I CAN'T TELL ONE OWNER FROM THE OTHER" EXCUSE

Dear Richard:

It's so frustrating: When I open my apartment door, my Siamese, Bangkok, darts between my legs, runs out into the hall, and, if my neighbor's door is open, scurries into his apartment. Why? Does she like him better? Is it because he owns old *Tom and Jerry* cartoons? I'm flummoxed. Maybe she wouldn't run off if I had either a bigger apartment or heavier legs. I know that cats are naturally curious, plus I heard that certain cats, called "Welcome Wagon" cats, were bred specifically to show up unannounced and annoy the neighbors. Could Bangkok be expressing some primal "I'm a free spirit and just not a slave to my mistress" urge?

*Jessica*

Dear Have You Ever Heard of
Cats Without Borders?:

Your cat should not have to be reminded that you're great. Be of good cheer, however, for you are not alone. Supposedly, Louis XVI's cat, Robespierre, was totally into the king, but each time Louis opened the front door of Versailles, Roby ran out to inspect the grounds, often venturing forth and appearing later at a nearby café, where he ordered *moules frites*. I hate to be the bearer of bad tidings, but be brave and face it: It would never occur to a cat to ask permission to go out, and rare is the cat able to resist an open door or window. Your problem is easily solved by carrying kitty around in a Snugli.

## IS YOUR CAT CHEATING ON YOU? PAY ATTENTION IF:

*1.* She takes a breath mint before leaving for a "playdate."
*2.* The moment you get home he no longer fetches your slippers.
*3.* He's lifting weights.
*4.* You see her cat carrier parked in front of a motel.
*5.* You come home unexpectedly and catch him with his tongue in a mouse's mouth.

## THE "MAYBE MY CAT HAS A TERRIFIC SENSE OF HUMOR" EXCUSE

Dear Richard:

As a birthday gift for Hamlet, my sister bought him a tiny sweatshirt that says, "I'm With Stupid." I never thought he'd wear it, but wear it he does, especially when we're together. My boyfriend says that Hamlet's not only being disloyal, but he's expressing his true feelings. I say that Hamlet's just having his little joke (he knows I love to laugh), and that he loves me and thinks I'm marvelous. What do you say?

*Jeannie*

Dear Report Immediately to the Principal's Office:

Your cat is having "his little joke"? Okay, I'm about to reveal the secret of all secrets: Except for one or two dyslexic Persians, who read poorly, cats can't read at all. If your sweater said "I'm With Stalin," he'd wear it, because—ready?—as long as it fits and complements his eyes, he doesn't care what it says. As far as expressing "true feelings," no cat on earth needs an "I'm With Stupid" sweater. Cats, even when they're naked, think they're smarter and superior to everyone—owners, dogs, royalty, and the Secretary of Defense.

## Chapter Eight

YOUR CAT'S JUST *NOT* THAT INTO YOU . . .

# If She Flaunts Her New Love Interest in Front of You

*If your cat were really into you she wouldn't let you know that she's slept with another cat's owner.*

You're all sappy for your cat and she doesn't reciprocate? You're crushed? Well, get in line behind the other 72,000,000 cat owners in the throes of cat-related romantic deprivation. Look, not to sound harsh, but the evolved owner knows that even if you've found your cat's G-spot, bugging her for affection is futile. Yes, cats bestow their love on their owners *when they're in the mood,* but cats are small and don't have that much love to give.

# A PEEK INTO KITTY'S BRAIN

| WHAT YOUR CAT IS DOING | WHAT YOUR CAT IS THINKING |
| --- | --- |
| **Kissing you** | Nice of you to shave your mustache, but I'm still just not that into you. |
| **Stalking your shawl** | I'll come when I'm ready. Right now very busy. What *is* this stupid garment? |
| **Studying self in mirror** | Does one cat deserve so much great bone structure? I'm more beautiful than ever. |
| **Primping** | Despite humidity, fur extra-beautiful. No wonder so many people love me. |
| **Yoga** | Seek liberation from material world but would kill for enlightenment and a lotus. |
| **Prowling Thanksgiving table when he thinks nobody's looking** | You're telling *moi* to scat??? It's not like *you* caught the turkey. |
| **Staring deeply into your eyes** | Wonder how *I'd* look in a blue yachting cap. |
| **Dozing in your lap** | Mmmm, scented bikini wax. |
| **Gazing longingly into your eyes as you eat calves' liver** | Want to be true to self, but am starving—must pretend, just this once, to be into owner. |
| **Expressing delight at your birthday gift to her** | Was I a chump to let this owner adopt me? |

# THE "BUT SECURITY WAS JUST DOING ITS JOB" EXCUSE

Dear Richard:

At the airport, before a recent flight, a screener conducted a pat-down of Butch, my cat. Not only did he not mind that a stranger was invading his "personal space," but he actually seemed to enjoy it. At one point, in fact, when Ms. Busy Hands began to frisk him, and, in my opinion, touch him inappropriately about the you-know-what, his eyes narrowed to slits and he began to purr. Afterward, when I returned him to his carrier, not only did he act as though nothing happened, he kept staring at my breasts! I'm really upset.

*Veronica*

Dear Five Minutes in the Time-Out Chair for You:

A little preflight fondling can be a good thing, especially if kitty is afraid of enclosed spaces. You sound a bit possessive, which is good for objects and spouses, but not for cats. You may recall that, according to anthropologist Margaret Mead, certain primitive South Seas societies had "community cats," bred for the express purpose of furnishing love to men who could prove they were starved for affection from their wives.

# Advisory to "Brokenhearted in Sacramento"

Stop whining because your cat has a girlfriend. Is he more into his girlfriend than you? Guess what: He's into neither of you. You can, however, still have a meaningful relationship with an adulterous cat as long as you don't get upset when he dyes his whiskers, disappears for days at a time, and comes home with a smile on his face.

## CAT PERSONAL

### TRULY UNCARING CAT.

Warm and sensuous on the outside, a cold little monster on the inside. Cruel Persian into major power trip (think a furry Goebbels), plus all the good things a well-appointed dungeon has to offer. Seeks master or mistress who desires domination, humiliation, and mortification. If you've always wanted to be abused while wearing a paper hat and sitting on a dunce stool, send a note to Bertram, c/o ASPCA for the Criminally Insane. Hours by appointment.

# THE "BUT THE DOG STARTED IT" EXCUSE

Dear Richard:

Yesterday afternoon, when Albert, my Yorkie, began to frantically hump my leg, my cat, Knuckles, jumped up and began to hump Albert. I know there's no excuse for this behavior, especially since Knuckles is bigger than Albert, but I think that Knuckles thought my leg was in danger and tried to protect me. What do you say?

*Trish*

Dear Failure to Understand the Concept of Hump and Dump:

A cat "protective" of its owner's leg, let alone its owner? Give me a break. Cats are pragmatic, taking their pleasure where they can, much like Henry VIII and Paris Hilton. It sounds to me like Albert and Knuckles really clicked. Why not go with it, bless the union, and don't confuse Albert by wearing bright-colored slacks.

## THE "LOVE, YOUR MAGIC SPELL IS EVERYWHERE" EXCUSE

Dear Richard:

I love my cat to pieces and I thought Chlorox loved me. Imagine how I felt the other morning while I was removing a tick from her fur, and she said, "Leave the tick alone. We're in love." I'm not the jealous type and I'm certainly not possessive, but this new romantic interest was a shocker. A tick? I know this is temporary (she gets crushes all the time, once on an exquisitely groomed shrew) and that she really cares for me. Is this a passing fancy? Should I protest now or wait until she regains her senses and starts being into me again?

*Denise*

Dear In Need of a Breath of Fresh Air:

Ticks are real heartbreakers, especially with cats. If it really is love, make sure the tick has honorable intentions. If not, give Chlorox plenty of time to heal before trying to renew your relationship.

Owners and their cats go through rough patches all the time, bickering over rights to the sofa cushion and who gets to sit closest to the radiator. She'll disappear for three days, then come home and think her absence is none of your business. You go on your honeymoon and she's really miffed because you left her with strangers? She claws the new wallpaper so you're not on speaking terms? Your cat met the tick of her dreams? Fine. But don't be a doormat. Let her know that instead of waiting around, you're going to go out and look for the love of *your* life. And that when you can't find it, you'll come back to her.

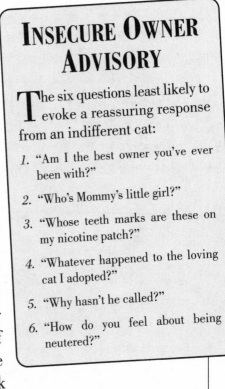

## INSECURE OWNER ADVISORY

The six questions least likely to evoke a reassuring response from an indifferent cat:

1. "Am I the best owner you've ever been with?"

2. "Who's Mommy's little girl?"

3. "Whose teeth marks are these on my nicotine patch?"

4. "Whatever happened to the loving cat I adopted?"

5. "Why hasn't he called?"

6. "How do you feel about being neutered?"

# THE "MAYBE I SHOULD DO MORE FOR HER" EXCUSE

Dear Richard:

I know cats also hate getting older, so for her ninth birthday I spent $3,000 on my wonderful Becky, a Russian Blue, so she could have her eyes done. Now she's so pleased with the results (the parrot calls her "bedroom eyes") that she wants a brow lift. I have no problem with the $5,000 it'll cost, but where does it stop? A nose job? Her tail liposuctioned? I really don't mind spending the money if that's what it takes to make her more that into me. Should I go for it?

*Harold*

P.S. I'm living in my car.

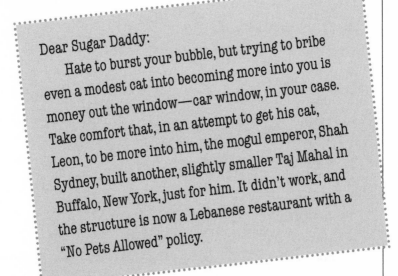

Dear Sugar Daddy:

Hate to burst your bubble, but trying to bribe even a modest cat into becoming more into you is money out the window—car window, in your case. Take comfort that, in an attempt to get his cat, Leon, to be more into him, the mogul emperor, Shah Sydney, built another, slightly smaller Taj Mahal in Buffalo, New York, just for him. It didn't work, and the structure is now a Lebanese restaurant with a "No Pets Allowed" policy.

## KITTY STATISTIC

A king-sized bed will sleep nine cats comfortably; eleven without the human.

# Cat Oxymora Test

Which two are not oxymora?

*1.* Has the hots for you . . . . . . . . . . . . . . . . . . . . . .cat

*2.* Law-abiding . . . . . . . . . . . . . . . . . . . . . . . . . . . . .cat

*3.* Deep-sea diving . . . . . . . . . . . . . . . . . . . . . . . . .cat

*4.* Awkward . . . . . . . . . . . . . . . . . . . . . . . . . . . . . . .cat

*5.* Spends all of her time trying to win you over . . . . .cat

*6.* Responds well to training . . . . . . . . . . . . . . . . . . .cat

*7.* Traitorous . . . . . . . . . . . . . . . . . . . . . . . . . . . . . . .cat

*8.* Slovenly . . . . . . . . . . . . . . . . . . . . . . . . . . . . . . . .cat

*9.* Obsequious . . . . . . . . . . . . . . . . . . . . . . . . . . . . ..cat

*10.* Cringing . . . . . . . . . . . . . . . . . . . . . . . . . . . . . . .cat

*11.* Volleyball playing . . . . . . . . . . . . . . . . . . . . . . . .cat

*12.* Barking . . . . . . . . . . . . . . . . . . . . . . . . . . . . . . . .cat

*13.* Homely . . . . . . . . . . . . . . . . . . . . . . . . . . . . . . . .cat

*14.* Regal . . . . . . . . . . . . . . . . . . . . . . . . . . . . . . . . . .cat

*15.* Mohair hating . . . . . . . . . . . . . . . . . . . . . . . . . . .cat

*16.* Dorky . . . . . . . . . . . . . . . . . . . . . . . . . . . . . . . . . .cat

*17.* Groveling . . . . . . . . . . . . . . . . . . . . . . . . . . . . . .cat

*18.* Putty in your hands . . . . . . . . . . . . . . . . . . . . . . .cat

*19.* Insomniac . . . . . . . . . . . . . . . . . . . . . . . . . . . . . .cat

*20.* Photogenic . . . . . . . . . . . . . . . . . . . . . . . . . . . . .cat

*21.* Riveted by Latin declensions . . . . . . . . . . . . . . . .cat

ANSWERS: 14 and 20. Unless your cat is a Hawaiian mix, then 3 is also correct.

## Chapter Nine

YOUR CAT'S JUST *NOT* THAT INTO YOU . . .

# If She Shows No Respect for You or Your Possessions

*You, dear owner, are far too materialistic.*
*Your shattered Hummel figurines were in my way.*

A cat who puts his needs ahead of yours? Impossible. A cat who weeps copious tears if she sheds on your sandwich or pees in the candy dish? (Thank you, L.J. of Iowa, for this invaluable bit of cat lore.) You wicked owner, what did you do to upset kitty? Look, cats can't really laugh at themselves. You have to do it for them. Instead of making excuses—"Oh, she can't get enough of me, so she chews on my mittens," or "When she digs her claws into my arm it means she's merely trying to reach my 'inner child'"—accept that cats are little kings and queens, accountable to no one except . . . well, you know who.

## THE "SUCH A CONSIDERATE KITTY, SHE DOESN'T WANT TO SHRED THE ENTIRE DRAPE" EXCUSE

Dear Richard:

Sometimes when she's feeling extra frisky or energetic or maybe (and I know I'm going out on a limb here) even craves attention, Brandy, my American Shorthair, runs over to the living room window and climbs up the drape. Then, instead of going all the way up and destroying the entire drape, she considerately stops halfway, clinging for dear life to the fabric until I come over and gently loosen the little sissy from the material. But instead of showing gratitude for her rescue with a tiny kiss or an appreciative lick, she leaps from my hands and darts away. If I pulled a drowning man out of the water, he'd at least buy me dinner. Is this Brandy's way of regaining her independence or is it that she's just a "scaredy-cat"?

*Elizabeth*

Dear Proud Owner of a Fabric Softener:

I'll break it to you gently. Although they manage to conceal it, cats spend much of their quality time agonizing over the fact that they're no taller than Toulouse-Lautrec. This is why they're constantly jumping on chairs, on sofas, and, if they've conquered their fear of heights, their owners' heads. It's the way these noble creatures compensate for spending their lives only inches from the floor (don't get me started on dachshunds). Do you deserve a more that-into-you, more so-glad-you're-my-savior cat? Of course. You also deserve, I'm sure, your own private jet. Next time she pulls that stunt, let her hang there for a day or two. She'll appreciate you more. Or less.

## CAT PERSONAL

### LOVE IT WHEN THE CAT'S GOT YOUR TONGUE?

I'm that cat. Killer head of hair, well-built (no stranger to Pilates), willowy, I'm a controlling tortoiseshell, fearless except for mice and confined spaces, interested in art, politics, having his scrotal sac rubbed, and fine dining. Seeks servile owner into hiking, sunsets, and leather. Just had teeth whitened.

**Reply to Fang, Box 3064.**

# THE "IT'S JUST THAT I LOVE YOU SO MUCH" EXCUSE

Dear Richard:

This is horrible, but I have to tell someone. The other morning, after a wonderful night of romance with my new sweetie, I was in the kitchen making breakfast. Oslo, my Norwegian Forest, whom I've had for four years, took a dump the size of Guam on my sleeping boyfriend. Luckily, Donny's a heavy sleeper and I was able to clean him up without waking him. And last week, when I got an "I love you" fax from Donny, Oslo climbed on the desk and threw up on it. I understand that cats can be very possessive and are notoriously territorial. Is Oslo trying to tell me something? Do you think he loves me more than he lets on? Do Oslo and I need to talk?

*Didi*

Dear Torn Between Two Loves:

If Oslo could talk, he'd say, "Frankly, my dear Didi, I don't give a damn. I don't have a jealous bone in my body, but I do occasionally enjoy a discreet and hopefully relaxing poo on a nice warm back, and really don't care whether the fax I toss my cookies on is from Donny or Louie's Pizza Parlor."

# READING KITTY'S TAIL POSITIONS

Thirteen signals cats make when running wild through the house, whether they're into you or not.

1. Abrupt lane change.

2. Stop tailgating.

3. Bong bong! U-turn alert!

4. Dead screech-to-a-halt stop (Wow! Who's that great-looking cat in the full-length mirror?)

5. Oops! Smashed vase from Aunt Clara. Not to worry, it was ugly.

6. No brakes! Running from the dog; he may be contagious. Thank God I'm faster than Seabiscuit.

7. Clear a path! Big game hunter after me.

8. Watch it! About to leap from table to sofa in a single bound.

9. Stand aside. Making hard left at doorway.

10. My bad. Knocked over snow globe. No wonder I suddenly feel chilly.

11. Sorry. Knocked over in-laws. Hey, maybe they'll leave sooner.

12. Emergency! Must reach kitty litter. Ate wasabi by mistake.

13. Gangway! Never learned to stop on Rollerblades.

## *Advisory to Ronnie*

Your love for your "almost human" cat is admirable, especially where you say she makes sure you're wearing your helmet when you bike, but it's not a good idea, when applying to an HMO, to put Maggie down as your next of kin. (Oh, and neither is mentioning Maggie on your resume as a reference.) Ronnie, just how lonely are you?

## THE "MAYBE SHE NEEDS HER OWN SPACE HEATER" EXCUSE

Dear Richard:

Sometimes I wonder whether my cat really loves me for me, or whether it's for the luxuries I provide. Here's what happens: Whenever I turn on my reading lamp and open my novel, my Angora, Femur, dashes over, lies down under the lamp, and not only hogs the heat (was not the halogen bulb invented just for cats?), but that big, giant body cuts off most of the light. If I gently try to move him, he opens his eyes, gives me that *screw off* expression that he learned at a Cat Owner Seminar for Cats, and goes back to sleep. Still, can't I safely assume that Femur is just trying to get a tan?

*Reggie*

Dear In Desperate Need of the Itty-Bitty Book Light:
From your brief letter, I suspect that your cat is so not that into you that he doesn't even help you turn the pages. Generally, cats hate cold. (Have you ever seen an Eskimo with a cat? I think not.) A cat is a heat-seeking missile, designed to seek out cozy, warm places that enable him to experience the adult minimum daily requirement of naps, which is 82.

# Quiz:
# Know Thy Kitty
# Terminology

**1. The term *vibrissa* refers to:**

 *a.* The song Venetian gondoliers sing when they're under-tipped

 *b.* A blend of catnip and muscatel

 *c.* A cat's whiskers

 *d.* A gourmet dish cooked by gypsies over an open manhole

 *e.* The newest Pentium chip

**2. *Persian Longhair* is:**

 *a.* A barbershop in Tehran

 *b.* An ayatollah with dreadlocks

 *c.* A cat so not into you that it meows in Arabic

 *d.* A Baghdad hippie

 *e.* A melon with hair

**3. *La Veille Chat* is:**

 *a.* A French wine made by fermenting berets

 *b.* A small wheel of Brie

 *c.* A Parisian cat with dentures

 *d.* The real name of Lipsy Fortunato

 *e.* A French holiday celebrating colon health

ANSWERS: 1. Either B or C is correct. 2. C. 3. Either A or C is correct.

# THE "IN HER PREVIOUS LIFE SHE MUST HAVE BEEN A BALLERINA" EXCUSE

Dear Richard:

I realize that cats have a lot of excess energy, but Rhett, my frisky Ragdoll, has it in abundance. I'm talking about a cat who, as though shot from a cannon, can suddenly blitz an entire apartment. With flaps lowered, Rhett starts "island hopping," taking off from the stool, executing a perfect four-point landing on the kitchen table, sliding past my oatmeal (upsetting the bowl), and then leaping on to the kitchen counter to refuel by raising his head for a quick gnaw on the hanging plant. When I tell him, "Stop that nonsense," he totally ignores me and continues to the top of the refrigerator, which he considers his "penthouse." When he's done, and without even a *sorry for the disturbance,* he quietly tiptoes out of the room and parks himself quietly by the living room window, as if nothing has happened. I love to watch him (he's so graceful), but I would think that if he was aware of the destruction he occasionally causes (my aunt's pre-Columbian shot glass is Rhett's latest casualty), he'd be more contrite.

*Rhonda*

Dear Seeker of Feline Damage Control:

Your first mistake is thinking that kitty has self-awareness. Your second mistake is thinking that your residence is a home instead of a vast gymnasium for . . . you guessed it: Rhett. It's part of the typical cat's charm, when he's feeling mischievous and extra-energetic, to turn a well-kept residence into an unnatural disaster zone. But it could be worse: It is not common knowledge, but there is a subspecies of cat found in the mid-Atlantic states called the V8 because of its incredible speed, power, and ability to leap tall bookcases in a single bound.

# TOUGH LOVE TIP

Even the most secure male is threatened when a woman lavishes more attention on her cat than she does on him. If you periodically blow kisses at tabby while you're making love, invite her to participate during a romantic moment in the Jacuzzi, and keep a photo of kitty twice the size of the photo of your boyfriend on your night table, you're sending a message: That you're more into the cat who's just not that into you than you're into the man who's totally that into you. Therefore, when your true love buys you something slinky and wonderful from Victoria's Secret, it's unwise to say, as you're opening his gift, "Nothing for my cat?"

# Are You a Trophy Owner?

Does your cat demand her breakfast on a tray? It's sad enough that your cat isn't that into you. Is she a gold digger too? Does she love you just for yourself? Does she see your inner beauty, your poetic soul, your warm, generous heart, and the way your eyes dance in the moonlight when she scratches you? Or does she allow you to own her for what you can give her? Renowned cat expert Olympia Deusenberg developed a list of the 13 telltale signs that you own a cat with an "agenda":

1. She's gorgeous.

2. When you enter a three-star restaurant you love the way she looks on your arm.

3. You're more than twice her age.

4. You earn 40 times what she did as a pole dancer.

5. She made it plain that she wants to be in your will.

6. She instantly stopped purring when you brought up a prenup.

7. She perks up when you take her to Rodeo Drive.

8. She demands that a sign reading *La Maison du Chat* be affixed to her Louis Vuitton cat carrier.

9. She refuses to sit on your lap unless you're wearing a) cashmere and b) her favorite scent.

10. She instantly lets you know you bought the wrong food by peeing on the Chinese rug once owned by Marco Polo.

11. More than once you've seen her flirt with the cable guy.

12. You're her fourth and richest owner.

13. She asked to be called "Prada."

## Chapter Ten

YOUR CAT'S JUST *NOT* THAT INTO YOU . . .

# If She Goes Out of Her Way to Make You Feel or Look Bad

*Your cat shouldn't shake her head and snicker when she sees you trying to squeeze into last year's bathing suit.*

Do cats really know when they're "out of line"? Look, as cat owners we're all struggling with a "Unified Cat Theory," one that would explain the connection between the gravitational and electromagnetic fields generated by drowsy cats and their refusal to knuckle under, no matter how obsequious the owner. Einstein couldn't do it, and he was working on the universe. Are cats uncaring? No. But their focus is on them: *Is this good for me? Is this making me warmer, more comfy? I'm so bored, why can't my owner be more amusing?* So next time you make an excuse, Oh, Jezebel would be more tender, more affectionate if only I _____ (fill in the blank), remember: she's a cat, you are her vassal.

## STRAIGHT FROM THE KITTY LITTER

**100** percent of cats polled said they've never been too busy to be just not that into an owner they were really not into. That does not mean, however, that cats are not attracted to their owners. Many cats, being independent, fear intimacy[1] and don't like to feel "owned." They hate when a loving owner bends over, looks into their eyes, and asks, "So, where is this relationship going?" It not only puts them on the spot, but they never quite know what to answer, especially if they don't want to hurt their owners' feelings.

---

[1] Even when they cuddle with you, a part of the cat's brain is thinking, *I hope my owner isn't getting any wrong ideas.*

# Official Kitty Horoscope

## (NOTE: ALL CATS ARE BORN UNDER THE SIGN OF SARDINIA)

*Your most attractive features:* Every inch of you and your insolence

*Turn-ons:* You love truth, needlepoint, and spacing out while staring in a shaving mirror

*Turnoffs:* Construction noise and cheap cuts of chicken

*Guilty pleasure:* Making yourself at home in the one room of the house you're forbidden to enter

*Ideal weekend menu:* Yogurt if you're feeling bloated; otherwise, a pig-out on General Tso's Smelts

*Recurring nightmare:* You get terminal diaper rash from the little pants your owner makes you model

*Favorite stress reliever:* Tossing your cookies on your owner's flip-flops

*Favorite indoor pastime:* Dozing

*Favorite outdoor pastime:* Napping

*Crash fitness program:* Doing a jackknife from top of armoire into the Jell-O

*Things you love most about your owner:* 1. Her innocence—she thinks you care when she calls you "Darling." 2. Her "Honk If You Love Abyssinians" bumper sticker

*Motto:* My Kingdom for Herring

# THE "BUT SHE MAKES HOUSE CALLS" EXCUSE

Dear Richard:

   For the past week I've been in bed with the flu, coughing, hardly able to breathe, and feeling like doo-doo. (No more barhopping without wearing a surgical mask.) I've tried everything: tea, aspirin, Tylenol, speed, coke. Nothing seems to work. My cat, Zebulon, has been of some comfort and I'm wondering: Do you think, although she's not that sympathetic to my illness (she has no problem whining if she's isn't fed on time), I'd heal faster by the laying on of paws? I read somewhere that the ancient Egyptians worshipped the healing power of cats and that, in the Fourth Dynasty, Pharaoh Nussbaum's herpes was magically eradicated by Kuff, the palace cat. What do you think?

*Aida*

Dear Can I Sell You the Brooklyn Bridge?:
Like vitamins and power bars, the medical benefits of "cat healing" have not yet been proven, although I am told that the FDA is holding clinical trials to determine whether certain hairless breeds can cure dyslexia. Maybe Zebulon is more into you than you think. If you can get her to hold still long enough, grab those little paws and try it, and let me know how it goes. I have a boil on my back.

# THE SIX THINGS . . .

Your cat wants to hear as he gets older:

1. "You're still a knockout."

2. "You haven't changed a bit."

3. "Of course you don't need a face-lift."

4. "You're still great in bed."

5. "You'll bury us all."

6. "Of course you're in the will."

# THE ONE THING . . .

A cat's owner doesn't want to hear as he gets older:

1. "Am I in your will?"

I leave
it all
to my
Kitty

# Advisory to Ramona

There could be several reasons Blossom, your Siamese applehead, nods off while you're telling her about your day:

1. She's narcoleptic. Rush her to the vet.
2. She's meditating.
3. She has an imaginary friend.
4. She's heard it a million times before.
5. She doesn't care that you had a rough commute.
6. She's deciding what she wants for Valentine's Day.

7. She's daydreaming about other things like:
   - Salmon croquettes.
   - Her ASPCA sweetheart.
   - Ham hocks.
8. She has no idea who you are.

# THE "BUT SHE'LL BE TRAUMATIZED FOR LIFE" EXCUSE

Dear Richard:

My husband and I are always fighting and I feel we've grown apart. We're no longer attracted to each other and we sleep in separate bedrooms. We've agreed on a divorce, but have decided to stay together until our emotionally fragile and extremely sensitive cat, Dim Sum, is fully grown.

What do you think?

*Greta*

Dear Greta:

I think you should heavily sedate her during the custody battle. Next question.

Cats aren't exactly lazy or uncaring, but they do tend to avoid labor-intensive tasks that interfere with their day. This precludes them from dispensing medical advice, Rolfing an owner with a bad back, and doing volunteer work like Meals-on-Wheels.

# Advisory to "From a Great House in Easthampton to a Double-Wide in Arkansas"

Bill, I'm sorry you lost your cat in the divorce, but when a judge asks a cat with whom it wants to live, the cat will inevitably choose the spouse who a) exudes the most heat, b) smells of fish, and c) she's most just not that into.

## STRAIGHT FROM THE KITTY LITTER

Constantly playing the sound track from *Cats* will not make your cat love you more. In fact, if she is sensitive or a graduate—even an insensitive one—of Juilliard, she may cover her ears with her paws and become even more not that into you. Musical tip: You can't go wrong with Aretha Franklin or Trini Lopez.

# THE "HEY, HE'S A CAT; THEREFORE HE'S ALLOWED TO BE TEMPERAMENTAL" EXCUSE

Dear Richard:

Here's the deal: When Twinkles was six months old, she was accidentally shut inside a refrigerator for several hours. When I finally found her, she seemed fine, except for a missing jar of pickled herring. Now, however, she refuses to go into her cat carrier, has to sleep with the light on, and if I don't say, "What a good Twinkles" exactly 30 times after she uses the kitty litter, she begins to mew pitifully. My boyfriend, the head pastry chef for PETA, suggests that the refrigerator incident was an emotionally shattering event, the cat is jittery, and that she needs to be on Paxil. I say, "Get over yourself, kitty, it's time to move on." Should I be more understanding?

*Elvira*

Dear Too Indulgent:

This sounds like a typical no-fault incident that your cat is milking. I knew a cat who'd been locked in a mailbox for several weeks; he subsisted on nothing but canceled stamps and hope, but emerged totally well-adjusted, except for a morbid fear of voting booths. I admit that it's tempting to feel sorry for Twinkles, but ask yourself: Are you sure she didn't shut herself inside the refrigerator just to get some privacy?

## Therapy Class 101:
# Healing After Heartbreak

When your cat breaks your heart it is permissible to:

1. Cry.

2. Lie in bed with a bottle of decent Chablis and two pounds of chocolate.

3. Hope in vain that kitty realizes what a catch you are (you love to laugh, are open to new adventures, and respect your cat as an individual).

4. Call a support group. (Cat Lovers Anonymous is always there for you. "Hi, my name is Zeke and I love my cat too much.")

5. Repeat this can't-fail mantra: "My cat will never love me, ommm, as much as, ommm, I love her." Repeat 40 times an hour.

Although the latest results of the Cat Genome Project show that feline and human chromosomes are shockingly similar, there are still important differences between you and your cat. Cats do not walk around thinking about competing, or winning at Scrabble, or feel threatened by other's success, or any of that stuff that plagues most humans (although a cat might experience *schadenfreude* if she sees the neighbor's hated dog carried off by a large bird). Nor do they ever sit down and wonder, "Am I worthy of my owner's love?" Cats are genetically hardwired to feel worthy of *everyone's* love. They are also hardwired to believe that no one is worthy of theirs.

# THE "MAYBE I'M USING THE WRONG FINGER" EXCUSE

Dear Richard:

Sometimes, when my cat annoys me, just to show him who's boss, I flip him off. I then get really frustrated when, instead of reacting appropriately (at least looking sheepish or putting his tail between his legs), he just sits there, continuing either to lick himself or he just turns and walks away. Is he a pacifist? Don't cats know when they're being insulted?

*Armand*

Dear Armand:

While you're at it, also try making faces at him and ordering him to stand in the corner. Now listen, my misguided cat lover, cats are pretty much immune to gestures and verbal discipline (although, once, in June of 1996, a farm cat in Ames, Iowa, urinated on a cow when his owner scowled at him). If you don't believe me, try this: The next time he extends his claws and jumps on your chest, knit your eyebrows, place your hands on your hips as you're standing in a puddle of your own blood, and say, "Bad cat, bad cat." Watch him cringe and assume a groveling position. Just kidding.

# THE "MAYBE SHE HATES TO SEE ME WIN" EXCUSE

Dear Richard:

I know cats hate boundaries and presume that, though *I'm* the one who pays the mortgage and taxes, the house is their domain. Okay, I refuse to argue with a cat. But the other night, when friends came over to play Scrabble, Cleo, my pudgy Abyssinian, jumped off the fireplace mantle, flew through the air and landed in the middle of the Scrabble board just as I had a seventy-five-point word. I was inconsolable, but after I stopped sobbing, my friends assured me it was just an accident. Maybe so, but I say Cleo was being competitive and probably felt threatened that I was about to achieve success. How else do you explain the fact that once, during a pinochle tournament, she peed all over my winning hand?

*Morris*

Dear Schlemiel:

That can be tough, particularly when you're sitting with those juicy Q and X tiles. But the good news is that cats are neither competitive nor destructive. Cleo's little head sees approximately one inch into the future and, whether it's leaping from a fence or walking the length of the sofa, her actions are unplanned (unless she hears her special can of food being opened). She is utterly indifferent to whether you win, lose, or draw. If she wasn't, she'd at least look at your opponents' hands and tell you what they have.

Don't let those pathetic meows fool you into thinking she's addressing you. Like most men, cats just like to hear themselves talk. And as with most men, cats' endless racket, even when seemingly directed at you, doesn't necessarily mean that they're, even for a nanosecond, that into you.

# CAT PERSONAL

## ARE YOU UNUSUAL?

Well, so am I. Poetry obsessed, sexually adventurous, enchanting tabby (Miss Fresh Step 2004), equally at home in high heels or little cat garters, wishes to humiliate, dominate, and shed all over an owner wearing wool and a clown wig. Love of the bizarre and midnight hayrides a must. I'll bring the manacles. Reply to Angie,

**Box 1006.**

## STRAIGHT FROM THE KITTY LITTER

**C**ats remain shrouded in fur and mystery, their state of mind often unreadable. Cat owners desperate for enlightenment, however, can easily gauge kitty's emotional state by forcing a mood ring on its paw, waiting a few moments, and then studying the color as follows:

| COLOR | MEANS | POSSIBLE REASON |
| --- | --- | --- |
| **Black** | *Crabby* | Owner playing Santana's *Greatest Hits* and humming along. |
| **Amber** | *Sad* | Still emotionally involved with previous owner. |
| **Blue** | *Happy* | Sun streaming through window, owner's lap soooooooooooo warm. |
| **Aqua** | *Happy, with reservations* | Finally adopted by loving owner but she has 27 other cats. |
| **Red** | *Angry* | Let go of my tail: I'm not a vacuum cleaner. |
| **Yellow** | *Paranoid* | Pretending everything's fine. but "certain" that mouse hole is haunted. |
| **Violet** | *Tense* | Found first crow's foot; also had a hot flash. |
| **Green** | *Stable* | Emotionally unavailable. |
| **Indigo** | *Concerned* | Owner using me as a fashion accessory; what happens when I'm suddenly last season's cat? |
| **Plaid** | *Upset* | Projectile vomiting, 10-year-old spinning me on a Lazy Susan. |

# THE "BUT SHE SEEMS SO LIGHT-FOOTED" EXCUSE

Dear Richard:

I tried to teach Lochinvar, my cat, the bolero, but instead of joining in the fun, she ran away and hid for several hours. I was astonished, since Locky is extraordinarily playful and usually up for anything—just the other day I dressed her in a tiny saffron-colored frock and we spent much of the afternoon playing Hari Krishna and (believe it or else) I'm *this close* to teaching her to select my dinner wine. I suspect that she loves me and wants to please me but has "resistance" to learning something new. What say you?

*Isabel*

Dear Instructor:

Well, while you're at it, why not teach her to moon walk? A recent poll, in fact, showed that, with the exception of the waltz, cats find dancing uncomfortable, especially if their owner is grasping their front paws and saying, "One two three, one two three." I suggest that you place her on your lap and, together, watch a DVD of *Singin' in the Rain*. I think you'll quite adore the way Donald O'Connor releases Lochinvar's Inner Kitty.

# Quiz: Know Thy Kitty

Think you know cats? Select the characteristic that best exemplifies the breed.

| A. CHARACTERISTIC | B. BREED |
|---|---|
| *1.* Poster child for arrogance. | *a.* Bengal |
| *2.* Never obeys first time summoned. | *b.* Siamese |
| *3.* Glib; can purr her way out of anything. | *c.* Himalayan |
| *4.* Courageous—will fish your retainer out of the Crock-Pot. | *d.* Tuxedo |
| *5.* Huge sense of entitlement. Sheds indiscriminately with no regard for allergies. | *e.* Tabby |
| *6.* Hot licking of owner's face deceives owner into thinking cat is affectionate. | *f.* American Shorthair |
| *7.* Always dignified and graceful. | *g.* Maine Coon |
| *8.* Keeps self immaculate. | *h.* Turkish Angora |
| *9.* Sometime Ice Queen. | *i.* Persian |
| *10.* Blissful naps a specialty. | *j.* Angora |
| *11.* A hunter and a gatherer. Thinks "edible panties" means exactly that. | *k.* Burmese |
| *12.* Unpredictable. | *l.* Abyssinian |
| *13.* Inherently lovable. | *m.* Egyptian Mau |
| *14.* Insulted if her name not featured on owner's car vanity plates. | *n.* Manx |
| *15.* Finicky eater, refuses to plea bargain. | *o.* Russian Blue |
| *16.* A terrible student of humility, but a great sleeping companion. | *p.* Scottish Fold |
| *17.* Will drop you like a bad habit for a shred of white chicken meat. | *q.* Tortoiseshell |
| *18.* Listens to her own inner voice: "Why can't I wear flip flops?" | *r.* Ragdoll |
| *19.* Leaps over tall armchairs; sayonara Precious Moment figurine. | *s.* Norwegian Forest |
| *20.* Sees germs humans can't. | *t.* Sphynx |

# RICHARD SMITH

Richard Smith, the writer-in residence, has written for several major publications, including *Cosmopolitan, The New York Times, Playboy,* and *Pravda.* His books include: *The Dieter's Guide to Weight Loss Before, During, and After Sex* (on which he lost 81 pounds during his busy season), *The Bronx Diet* (on which he lost ½ pound), *The Newlyweds' Guide to Sex on the First Night* (during which he gained 22 pounds), several *365 Days and Nights of Sex* calendars, and *Love Muscle of Durango* (a gourmet cookbook). A skilled cat lover and talk show guest, he has made over 100 television appearances throughout the country. He becomes especially entertaining when his book is displayed. He likes hiking, camping, fine dining, concerts, and agriculture.

David Sipress is a regular contributor to *The New Yorker* and the author of eight books of cartoons.